LOSING YOUR RELIGION, FINDING YOUR FAITH: SPIRITUALITY FOR YOUNG ADULTS

Brett C. Hoover

PAULIST PRESS
New York/Mahwah, N.J.

Scripture used in this book came from the *New Revised Standard Version* and the *New American Bible.*

Cover design by Irving Freeman

Interior design by Joseph E. Petta

Copyright © 1998 by The Missionary Society of St. Paul the Apostle in the State of New York

Library of Congress Cataloging-in-Publication Data

Hoover, Brett.
    Losing your religion, finding your faith : spirituality for young adults / by Brett C. Hoover.
        p.   cm.
    Includes bibliographical references.
    ISBN 0-8091-3782-8 (alk. paper)
    1. Young adults—Religious life. 2. Spirituality—Catholic Church. I. Title.
BX2355.H58   1998
248.8´4—dc21   97-35323
                                                                                CIP

Published by Paulist Press
997 Macarthur Boulevard
Mahwah, New Jersey 07430

Printed and bound in the
United States of America

Contents

INTRODUCTION: Losing Your Religion   1

1. Spirituality   9

2. The Spiritual Road Trip   13

3. Getting Out of the Garage—
   Commitment and the Spiritual Journey   22

4. Scams of Faith—Losing Our Spiritual Myths   42

5. Balancing Our Burdens   53

6. Keeping Our Eye on the Ball—Dealing with the
   Distractions of Young Adulthood   65

7. Transforming Our Expectations   80

8. Spiritual Supplies   87

9. Companions in Faith   98

10. Accoutrements of a Mature Faith   115

11. Discernment—Mapping My Road of Faith   126

12. Conclusion—Editing God In   137

NOTES   145

APPENDIX   147

READINGS ON CODEPENDENCE AND ADDICTION   149

Acknowledgments

This book began around the dining room table at St. Mark's University Parish in Santa Barbara, California. A group of young adults wrote and reflected about spirituality with the encouragement (and prodding) of two Paulist priests. The book has evolved greatly since then, but a chunk of what is here comes from that dining room conversation. Thus, I am first grateful to those who formed that group:

> Lorena Duncan
> Fr. Bill Edens, C.S.P.
> Teresa Fanucchi
> Paul Hicks
> Kathy Murray
> Fr. Ken McGuire, C.S.P.

I am also indebted to those who, over time, read this thing over and offered corrections and suggestions. They include Don Schwartz, Ken McGuire, Warren Holmes, Beth Shively, and Bill Edens. A small cadre of unknown young adults chosen by my editor, Larry Boadt, also made some wonderful suggestions for the final draft.

This book is dedicated with love to my first spiritual teachers, my Mom and Dad.

Introduction: LOSING YOUR RELIGION

"I've lost my faith," she said to me firmly. "I just can't believe in all that stuff any more." She was staring at me intently, waiting for my response. After all, I was her church-going friend. I was supposed to have all the answers. Only I didn't.

When I asked her to tell me what had happened, why she had lost her faith, she gave me a list of seemingly disconnected facts. Her boyfriend's mother had died unexpectedly of cancer despite her fervent prayers. Church was boring. Her astronomy teacher's account of the Big Bang made a whole lot more sense than God's creating the universe in seven days. What about evolution? Furthermore, her mother was always telling her not to have sex before she was married because the church says it's a sin. With all the violence and injustice in the world, why was the church always talking about sex? Because of these things, she had lost her faith.

This upset me. Could a person really lose her faith? Was she now an atheist? Was I being silly or childish for continuing to believe?

✝

Losing my faith. It almost sounds silly, as if faith could be misplaced. Have you seen my faith? I've been tearing the house apart looking for it. But it's not silly at all. It's a common and often painful experience for young adults. Suddenly there is confusion where there was certainty, often resulting in tensions in relationships with parents and friends. It's no fun to lose your faith. Yet it is a critically important part of *growing* in faith, even if that sounds like a contradiction.

Losing my faith *is* a matter of misplacing something. We put our faith, our trust, in a particular way of looking at God and the world, and that viewpoint fails us. For young adults, most of us have put our faith in the brand of religion we learned when we were young. A simple kind of religion, it boasts black-and-white answers for the big questions of life. It ignores the great problems of suffering and evil, of how to interpret the Bible, of the human fallibility of the church itself, of the complications of living a moral life. This religious vision works well for children and even for many teenagers, but it does not measure up to adult expectations. As Saint Paul said, "When I was a child, I spoke like a child, I thought like a child, I reasoned like a child; when I became an adult, I put an end to childish ways" (1 Cor 13:11). Childhood faith is good for children; they need things presented with simplicity. But such a viewpoint eventually has to fail an adult. Young adults really have no choice but to "lose their faith."

This is a bit of a misnomer, however. We don't really lose our faith—not, that is, our trust in the God who is beyond our comprehension. We have simply *misplaced* our faith, put our faith in a religious system that ultimately did not cut the mustard. It wasn't our fault, and it was pretty much inevitable. What we truly lost was our *religion,* our humanly invented way of looking at God and at the world. Losing our religion is part and parcel of the lifelong process of spiritual growth.

What made sense at fifteen will not make sense at twenty. In the same way, what made sense at twenty will not fit our life experience at thirty-five. And so on. Spiritual growth is always a process of learning and then letting go, of losing our religion and finding our faith again.

So it has happened for all the great religious figures of history. Young Saul of Tarsus (St. Paul) thought he understood all that his faith required of him, only to find that God had called him to join with those he had zealously persecuted "in God's name." The Buddha was raised with the customary religious training of ancient India; but his meeting with a sick person, an old person, and a corpse changed his point of view forever. He left behind the way of life he had been taught to hold sacred in order to seek enlightenment. In more recent times, the young writer Thomas Merton joined a monastery in the 1940s, seeking to escape the terrible world. Years later he found that his contemplative life was drawing him to a new concern for the very world he had forsaken. Thus, he became a well-known spokesperson for justice and peace issues in the 1960s.

Even Jesus, it seems, had to lose his religion. I do not mean his Judaism. Jesus was a faithful Jew until the day he died. His view of the way God was acting in his life, however, changed radically. As a young man, presumably thinking like everyone else that repentance and a new beginning were the way to be ready for the coming of God's kingdom, he sought to be baptized by John. But as he emerged from the water, the Holy Spirit came upon him, designating him as the *instrument* of God's reign. From that moment, his life would be entirely different. God's call would lead him to proclaim the establishment of a kingdom not at all according to traditional expectations.

Important Note: Jesus did not lose his Judaism; he found a new way to understand it. Faith grows as religion is lost and found again. The "found again" part is important. Our response to God in faith always happens in the context of religion (even if it's not an organized religion). We are not God, and we have no choice but to understand and trust God in our human ways. They are good but limited ways. The reason most people opt to understand their faith in the context of some version of organized religion is that there is safety in numbers. As a community, we're smarter than each of us is on his or her own. We have the wisdom of those who came before us on which to depend. In our individualistic society, many people believe that only what the individual experiences is real. Thus, what I experience is pure, unadulterated faith, as opposed to that faulty organized religion stuff. Now, organized religion *is* faulty, to be sure! No human institution is perfect, even as we believe God is with us to keep us from going permanently astray. But neither is any individual perfect. Our "individual religion" has just as much (if not more) chance for messing up God's revelation in our lives.

In any case, although for most of us losing our religion does not have the drama of the stories above, it remains crucial to our attaining a mature faith. Below are a few composite stories, tales of young adult spirituality that are actually (except for the last one) several people's stories mixed together.

✝

Karen was the first in her large and traditional family to go away to college. She was twenty, having already attended the local community college. While living at home, she always went to church—it was expected of everyone living under her parents' roof. When she went away to college, however, Karen stopped attending. At first, she didn't know where the church was. Later, she had a lot of studying to do. Finally, she began to admit to herself what was really happening. For the first time in her life, it was her decision, and she did not want to go. It's not that she didn't believe in God, she told herself.

But the old-fashioned way of talking, the boring sermons, the strict rules about sex and other things just didn't seem to make sense anymore. She wanted to experiment in her new environment, enjoy the change of scenery. She was still the same person, of course, but she needed time to decide for herself.

Rachel's story unfolds in a different direction. She grew up "vaguely religious" in a Protestant denomination. Her family would sometimes attend the local church, but that practice became less frequent as Rachel and her sister grew older. Finally, by the time Rachel was a teenager, her mother stopped attending church altogether. They rarely discussed religion, and Rachel was too busy with school and activities to think about it anyway. Several years later, when Rachel was about twenty-six, the topic came up again when she discovered that her new boyfriend came from a very devout family. Rachel did not feel particularly drawn to attending church, but she did realize that she still believed in God, and that spirituality was important to her.

Leticia had a different but also common experience. She was raised Roman Catholic, and she went to church every Sunday of her life. At eighteen she began attending the local state university while she lived at home. There she ran into Patrick, a member of a campus Bible study group. He invited her to attend the group, and she welcomed the chance to form some new friendships on that huge and intimidating campus. Leticia had a limited amount of knowledge about the Bible, but the things her companions were showing her there seemed to conflict with her Catholic upbringing. Finally, much to her parents' horror, she started attending a local Protestant evangelical church. She began to feel very conflicted, having a certain fondness for Catholic traditions and for her old Catholic friends and yet a burning enthusiasm for her new community and the new friends she wanted so much to please.

On the other side of the spectrum is my own story. Like Leticia and Karen, I grew up in a very religious household, steeped in faith and church from a very young age. When I eventually left home for college, I still went to church. Yet gradually questions wandered into my head. Not everything I'd been taught as a child was making sense. Was everything about sex and the body as sinful as I had presumed? Who was I to tell other people that their religions weren't true? How could Jesus really be God and a human being too? The old simple answers were not holding up for me. Luckily, I had several friends, some teachers, and a couple of priests who accepted and encouraged my need to question. They seemed to understand intuitively that "losing religion" was a part of growing in faith. So I kept searching and asking questions, still interacting with a community of faith and tapping the wisdom of old religious traditions and committed believers. Eventually, I grew (that is, am growing) into a more mature faith.

In all these stories, there is a losing of religion. The package of stories and beliefs of younger days ultimately fails to satisfy these young adults. But losing our religion is only the beginning of a process of finding mature faith, a process of growth and development. All of the young adults described continued to hang on to a sense of the divine, the sense that a Mystery greater than ourselves, indeed greater than the religion of our youth, was ever present and at the center of our reality. All of them were and probably still are groping their way toward that Holy Mystery, even though at different speeds and in different ways. A couple of them were fortunate enough to have some support and guidance. (It is much more difficult to proceed without that.) Yet all were beginning the process of discovering their own mature faith.

Losing our religion is not the end of our faith, or even of our religion. It is a gateway to a new journey for most of us, a trip on the "road of faith." It's a complicated and even dangerous road, but a richly rewarding one as well. This book is about young adult spirituality, about the journey from losing our religion to finding our faith. My hope, and the hope of those who helped prepare this book, is that you, the reader, will find here some insights and stories that correspond to your experience on your own road of faith.

Chapter One: SPIRITUALITY

What is spirituality? A book about young adult spirituality has to work up some kind of understanding of what spirituality is. This is the sort of request that elicits responses like, "Well, um, it's...uh, well..." or "Spirituality is dealing with spiritual things." These responses tell us nothing—except, perhaps, that we are not exactly certain what it is. We don't have a quick and easy definition at our fingertips.

With time and thought, of course, ideas come to mind. I have collected a few below.

Spirituality is:
+ The glue that binds all things together
+ The meaning and richness in life
+ Trying to see things in the big picture
+ Uncovering reality and God's will for us
+ Not a supernatural realm though it does include more than what we can touch and see
+ The kingdom of God, a dream for a better world

+ Living in relationship with God, with other people, and with all of Creation
+ Not tomorrow or yesterday but today, this moment, now
+ Getting in touch with ourselves that we might get in touch with each other.

Saddled now with too many answers instead of too few, we grow confused. What is spirituality? Clearly, it is a complicated thing and cannot be so precisely defined. It is Mystery! How do we talk about mystery? Faced with such richness and complexity, we turn to stories.

Spirituality and Storytelling

Spirituality is like the ocean. From the side of the cliff, we look out and see unintelligible vastness. We know certain things about it, generalities that so-called experts have told us. But looking over it from our proverbial cliff, our eyes can tell us very little. We ask ourselves: *What can I really say about this awesome and frightening body?* Stories, then, are the floor windows on the glass-bottom boats we use to explore the ocean of spirituality (alert! metaphor being stretched thin). We come down from our cliff, climb aboard, and peer down through these windows. We peek into mystery. We see spirituality from new and penetrating angles. We absorb previously unavailable information, and we test the knowledge given to us by the experts.

Stories are also like prisms. Simple though they are, they take the complicated but integrated light of spirituality and split it into its component colors. In other words, they can communicate many levels of truth in a simple framework. Consider the children's story of the race between the tortoise and the hare. That story tells children much more about life than simply saying to them, "Sometimes things do not turn out as you would expect." Think of the recovering alcoholic who stands up at an Alcoholics Anonymous meeting and tells his or her story. Doesn't that say much more to a crowd of drinkers than standing before them and telling them not to drink because it will ruin their lives?

Christians have always known that stories were the windows into spirituality. The earliest disciples heard Jesus speak to them in parables, simple stories from their everyday experience that were nonetheless rich in common sense. The early church passed these stories down by word of mouth through great preachers like St. Paul. Many years later, people began to record in writing the stories they had heard of the life of Jesus. Over another century or two, the telling of stories became ritualized. That tradition remains to this day, for why do Christians gather on Sundays but to share and enact stories from the life of Jesus of Nazareth? What are the Scriptures but collections of stories about people's relationship with God?

Personal Storytelling

To discover spirituality, we have to delve into stories, but not merely stories about Jesus. Spirituality asks that we look into our *own* stories. Strewn across our lives are the lessons and insights that form the personal spiritual libraries of each of us, and those will only be uncovered in the telling of our personal stories. Socrates tells us that "the unexamined life is not worth living," and we Christians trust in this piece of wisdom. Looking at our lives with the eyes of faith, we find out what makes us tick, where we are in our relationship with God, and where we might be going.

Telling our own stories has other benefits as well. It situates us in time, place, and tradition. It pinpoints where we fit into the world by connecting us to family, culture, and religious traditions. We learn about who we are by examining where we came from. We take out the storytelling spools of the past and unravel the yarn of our lives. We uncover what it meant to grow up where we did, with whom we did, and under the conditions we did. One friend tells me stories of how his father instilled in him great pride in his Italian heritage and Catholic faith. Another recreates events from days in a private Anglican boys school in Canada. These stories tell both them and me much about themselves. The insights involved may seem to have little to do with spirituality, but they do, for spirituality is the putting together of all the parts of our lives with the eyes of faith.

II

Chapter Two: THE SPIRITUAL ROAD TRIP

In between losing your religion and finding your faith is a journey. All the great mystics and saints agree: Life is a series of spiritual journeys. Thus, for young adults the process of losing their religion and finding their faith is a species of journey. However, since *journey* is a vague term to us modern folk, let us think of it as a series of road trips.

When I think of a road trip, I recall a particular trip I took in the summer of 1989 from Santa Barbara, California, to Vancouver, British Columbia. Three friends and I packed ourselves and our supplies into a Mazda and wandered up the coast. We drove through the days, stopping frequently to take in beautiful views and unusual sights. Along the way we had long conversations, sharing thoughts and feelings, sometimes of a profound nature, sometimes silly and trivial. At night we would camp out, singing contemporary songs along with a guitar. It was a wonderful trip, full of laughter and learning.

Two things stand out when I recall that trip. The first is that the journey itself was more important and more fun than getting there. Although we enjoyed Vancouver, I don't think the trip would have been much diminished if we had decided to turn around ten miles before we reached the city limits. Second, I learned much about myself and about life on that trip. While we navigated our way through new territory, I charted a course through unfamiliar inner terrain. Something about going to strange places, meeting new people, and living closely with a small group of people directs a person into self-exploration.

What then characterizes spiritual road trips, the metaphorical travels down the road of faith that comprise our lives? Do they have destinations? Are there passengers? Directions? Maps? How long does it take to complete these journeys?

If this book were being written from the perspective of the "old religion"—that is, the faith of younger days—I might begin by giving precise answers to the above questions. The journey is to God; the Bible (or some authority figure) is the map; stick closely to the prescribed route and you won't take a wrong turn and end up on the Road to Hell (a major crossroad on the road of faith, evidently paved with good intentions). While you are driving, keep your eyes on the road ahead of you. And for God's sake, don't stop until you get there.

For better or for worse, this book is not being written from such a perspective. From our perspective, the destination of any of the many spiritual road trips of life is still living with God, but that is not so supernaturally understood. Most of the living with God that concerns us occurs firmly on the ground while we are still alive. About what happens after that, we have only limited information. As for the maps—well, we still have maps, signposts, navigators, of course. But the routes are not so fixed; we are allowed side trips. We do not travel alone. And furthermore, we are counseled to enjoy ourselves. These road trips, like their literal counterparts, are rich explorations of ourselves, God, and one another. They are full of laughter and learning. In fact, you could say that the destination, our living with God, is the outcome of these learnings and explorations, the changes within us that are produced. In this manner, we make our way toward finding our mature faith.

The Spiritual Journey Is Not a Commute

Spiritual Faux Pas: Imagining that we are to commute down the road of faith.

Although the aforementioned saints and mystics refer to life as a spiritual *journey,* there is a noticeable lack of accounts of life as a spiritual *commute.* This is not merely because many of these people (though not all, by any account) lived before anyone had ever imagined living twenty miles from one's job. In a commute, the sole objective is reaching one's destination. I get in my car, turn on the traffic report, pull onto the freeway, and get there. You never hear someone say, "Well, I took the job because I wanted to enjoy that extra half-hour commute." Commuters are goal-oriented travelers.

On the road of faith, fundamentalist Christians are the commuters. They are simply on this earth to get to God in heaven after earthly life is over. Thus, their focus is otherworldly. What they do along the way is only important if it contributes to this goal; whether or not they enjoy the ride is not pertinent. The richness of the spiritual life along the way is irrelevant, merely a distraction. The purpose of life is to get there, "there" being salvation in the afterlife.

But our saints, mystics, and spiritual directors speak not of the commute, but of the journey or road trip. Why? Well, as we have said, the important thing about a road trip is not so much where I am going as what happens along the way. In a sense, on a road trip I am going every place along the route to my official destination. This turns out to be a great metaphor for the spiritual life. The spiritual life has as its goal or destination *living* with God. The well-rounded Christian, however, knows that God is not merely in heaven; God is present everywhere in our lives. On the road of faith, God is every place along the way. If we look for God only at the end of the line, in heaven, we miss out! We miss out on the wonders of God in nature, in the love between two people, in the service of one committed to helping people, in laughter and art and all the thousand little ways God comes to us throughout one day in our lives. The wisdom of the ages cries out for living in the now, not merely bearing life as it is until we find our heavenly reward.

The Divine Trip-tik

Necessary to the idea of a spiritual road trip is the plan behind it. Our spiritual journeys are not random jaunts through the back roads of life. "Before I formed you in the womb, I knew you," God tells the prophet Jeremiah; "before you were born I consecrated you" (Jer 1:5). For each of us, God is hatching a plan, a spiritual itinerary not unlike the auto club's famous "trip-tik." Not set in stone, the plan grows as we grow. It is our lifelong task to cooperate with God in developing and uncovering our "travel plan." To do this, we try to discern and understand the entreaties and guidance of the Holy Spirit, who is navigator on this road of faith. More on that later.

Company on the Road: Community, Tradition, Scripture

Many of the saints, mystics, and spiritual directors of today have pointed out a fundamental spiritual error of contemporary Western culture. The error is most commonly known as individualism. Somewhere in the basement of our consciousness dwells the idea that we are supposed to make life's road trips on our own, solo, without assistance or company. At some point during the birthing of modern Western culture, the notion crept into our heads that the primary unit of reality is the individual and that all truth, morality, wisdom, and meaning in life exist only within that individual. This has had beneficial consequences in the Western world; for instance, we now champion individual human rights and freedoms. However, there have been negative results as well. The importance of community, originally constituted by the village or small town, has waned considerably. In its place exists an unrealistic self-reliance as well as isolation and alienation.

This concept of absolute self-sufficiency flies in the face of time-tested spiritual wisdom. Without community on the road of faith, the lone traveler misses out on the input of fellow travelers. He or she never benefits from the creative frenzy that a brainstorming group can provide. Who wants to go it alone, anyway? Traveling the road of faith with others is more fun, if nothing else. But most of all, we travel together because that is our nature. Human beings are designed to conduct their lives in community, whether it be the community of family, town, club, or faith. Individualism is not just a poor alternative; it is a lie. People are built to be interdependent, and at our best, we seek each other's support and assistance on the road of faith. Relationship is critical to the spiritual life.

In our Christian tradition, the wisdom and input of the community comes to us both through the channels of history and direct from the Christian community alive today. We speak of Tradition and scripture as historical records of community. The earliest Christians gathered their experience of the Christ into what we now refer to as the New Testament. Their spiritual wisdom still rings true today, and we turn to the scriptures to help us grow and develop. In addition, by oral and written history we have the wisdom of twenty centuries of Christianity, derived from the Christian community's long struggle with difficult questions. This we call *Tradition*. We use it along with scripture to discern whether the spiritual giants of the past centuries have dealt with the situations we face today. Why should we make the same mistakes they did all over again? God's people have seen fit to pass on their experiences over the centuries so that we might continue to grow and expand on them today.

It is helpful for Christians in an individualistic society to recall that the community itself—whether it be parish, city, church, or world—is on a spiritual journey. We are participants in these communal sojourns down the road of faith. Just as the Spirit calls the faith community to help the individual to grow spiritually, so it is the responsibility of the individual to help the community grow and move forward on this spiritual road trip. Thus, we are reminded of our responsibility to one another. We are called upon to build a more just society. God asks for our complete attention and cooperation in the effort to move our world community down the road of faith to its ultimate destination—the kingdom of God!

Discipline—Motor Oil for the Road of Faith?

To get a driver's license in Germany, you have to be able to perform elementary maintenance and repairs on your car. The Germans realize that crucial to the success of any road trip (or commute, for that matter) is the matter of keeping your automobile running properly. If we wish to travel, we have to ensure that there is sufficient gasoline, oil, brake fluid, automatic transmission fluid, and radiator water for smooth and healthy operation. Otherwise, we could find our road trip interrupted by an unpleasant breakdown.

The spiritual life is no different. We have to keep our vehicles in shape. My vehicle on the spiritual road trip is *me*. So I have to keep me in shape physically, emotionally, and mentally. As a spiritual journeyer, I need to eat right, exercise, spend time with friends, think, cry, laugh, share, love, and pray. I need to know the signs that my "vehicle" is breaking down—fatigue, emotional stress, and so forth. The spiritual life asks that we be regularly attuned to the needs of body, mind, heart, and spirit. That requires discipline. Discipline is the motor oil of the road of faith. It keeps everything running smoothly.

The person who shows no discipline but only acts as he or she feels at any particular moment can never get very far on the road of faith. The spiritual journey requires an act of the will. Discipline strikes us as difficult at times; it may even be a bad word to some. The good news is that as we grow, many of the disciplines we practice out of duty become either unconscious habits or things we actually want to do.

The Mentor—Mechanic and Consultant

The spiritual experts of most of our human traditions agree on the need for a spiritual journeyer to have a wise and supportive mentor or spiritual companion, a person of experience to advise and assist the young journeyer on his way. Scripture concurs. The books of First and Second Kings explain how Elisha receives prophetic power and wisdom through the guiding influence of the great prophet Elijah. Even movies and literature concur. Consider that Luke Skywalker had his Yoda; King Arthur, his Merlin; and Carlos Castenada, his Don Juan.

But isn't the mentor a mythical character of days gone by, not needed for today's spiritual road trip? Not so. Along today's road of faith, the mentor continues to serve as mechanic and spiritual consultant, helping us to find the right questions, directions, and maps to keep ourselves in shape on our unique path down the road of faith. We resist mentoring, perhaps out of individualism. Some long to maintain the illusion that they can travel the road of faith without any assistance. In our society, we seem to resist community itself, let alone a special member of that community whose job it is to help guide us. Yet these spiritual companions are critical to our journeys. Our best navigating of the road ahead requires their services, whether they be licensed spiritual directors, ministers, professors, nuns, priests, or just wise people of experience that we come to know. As the book of Tobit says, "Seek counsel from every wise person, and do not think lightly of any advice that can be useful" (Tb 4:18).

The Navigator—The Holy Spirit of Truth

"I will ask the Father, and he will give you another Advocate to be with you forever. This is the Spirit of truth" (Jn 14:16–17).

Fortunately, as we road trip through young adulthood (and through life), we do not have to depend exclusively on any earthly guide. Jesus promised us the Spirit, a celestial navigator to be with us always. Christians have always tried to follow the leading of the Spirit. For example, in the Acts of the Apostles, the writer describes the situation thus: "When they came opposite Mysia, they attempted to go on into Bithynia, but the Spirit of Jesus did not allow them; so passing by Mysia, they went down to Troas" (Acts 16:7–8).

We still respond to the directions of the Spirit in our lives today. We recognize that the Holy Spirit moves with us and directs various persons, events, thoughts, and feelings into our lives. These things not only announce the constant presence of God in our lives, but they serve as signposts on the road of faith as well, showing us shortcuts or letting us know when we have made a wrong turn. We can think of these signposts and messages from the Holy Spirit as divine Post-its (in honor of that little yellow stick-em-up pad that has become such a mainstay of communication in our society). These messages are little reminders, hints for the road of faith. In a time of great self-doubt, a note of praise from a friend could be a Post-it from the nurturing Spirit of God, restoring my self-confidence. An awe-inspiring sunset could indicate to me that appreciation of nature is a way for me to pray. The heartfelt words of a song or a verse of scripture might answer a question. Many believe that messages from the Spirit may be found by deciphering recurring life patterns or using other psychological tools.

We must remember that the Holy Spirit does not merely send us soothing greeting-card-type messages. God the Holy Spirit loves us enough to give us bad news when we need to hear it. Who among us has not heard the voice of God in the friend who calls to tell us to get our act together? I might hear the Spirit in my boss complaining about the quality of my work. These are difficult messages to receive, but if we respond to them, they can improve the quality of our lives and move us a few miles down the road of faith.

The key to letting our celestial navigator work in our lives is to be open to Post-its. God speaks to us constantly every day in every week. The influence of the Spirit buzzes around us. We serve ourselves best when we unlearn our defenses against the Spirit (our illusions of self-sufficiency and total independence) and learn how to read the signs of God's guidance and love that the Spirit brings to us.

III

Chapter Three: GETTING OUT OF THE GARAGE—COMMITMENT AND THE SPIRITUAL JOURNEY

> Now the Lord said to Abram, "Go from your country and your kindred and your father's house to the land that I will show you. I will make of you a great nation, and I will bless you, and make your name great, so that you will be a blessing. I will bless those who bless you, and the one who curses you I will curse; and in you all the families of the earth shall be blessed." So Abram went, as the Lord had told him. (Gn 12:1–4)

Faith requires commitment. The great spiritual stories, old and new, attest to this. Abraham (then called Abram) was called into a special faith relationship with God. He responded by committing himself to the journey God had proposed, and he remained committed to trusting in God throughout his ensuing adventures. Countless blessings were poured upon Abraham and his wife Sarah, and they became the parents of many nations.

Just as Abraham's spiritual journey flourished as a result of

God's grace and Abraham's commitment to God, so it is for every human being. Countless other stories recall the theme. Sensing a call from God, the sixteenth–century saint Ignatius of Loyola determined to set out on a pilgrimage, and no one could dissuade him. Jesus himself realized the need for commitment, that "he must go to Jerusalem" (Mt 16:21) if he were to truly be messiah and prophet as was his call. Even in contemporary stories, the theme of commitment remains. Consider Luke Skywalker in the famous *Star Wars* movies. This young spiritual hero realizes that if he is to be a Jedi Knight, he must commit himself to difficult training in the Force under that greenest of spiritual masters, Yoda.

Faith requires commitment if it is to develop and grow. Yet young adulthood is the time when, stereotypically at least, people have the most trouble with commitment. Buoyant in the freedom of losing the old religion that weighed us down, we might neglect to begin the search anew. Or perhaps we balk at leaving behind the familiar routine for a new quest. For whatever reason, we avoid that commitment that brings us important spiritual supplies, focus, and the power to choose. To return to our road trip metaphor, we stall before we have even left the garage. Perhaps we are waiting for our fear, misgivings, or indecision to go away. Waiting for such things, however, is like waiting for the end of the world. We could be waiting a long time.

How then to proceed? What is it exactly that delays us? First let's take a look at some concrete examples of this "stalling."

Fear of Commitment: Scenes from Real Life

Perhaps these situations sound familiar:

+ A twenty-three-year-old woman held five full-time jobs in the space of one year.

+ A college freshman started working as a reporter for the college newspaper, wrote one story, and then mysteriously never got around to writing another.

+ A twenty-eight-year-old stated, "Well, I believe in all religions," but refused to take any of them seriously enough to practice it.

+ A college junior was urged by his professor to begin a research paper at least several weeks before the due date. He began work on it two days before.

+ A young military man found himself moving about the country, yet he never made an effort to keep in touch with friends he left behind.

These types of situations are common experiences for young adults, and it would be severe and hypocritical to begin making condemnations (ask me how long it took before I really got down to writing this book). Furthermore, these experiences do not seem, at first, to be critical to spiritual life. Yet they are. A woman who "believes in all religions" but never commits to one is like an athlete who loves sports but never decides on one in which to train herself. She will not grow as an athlete until she chooses. Likewise, a man who loses touch with all his former friends as he moves around the country misses a rich opportunity. It is chiefly through the significant others in our lives that we experience God and grow spiritually. In other words, a refusal to develop friendships over time is a way of locking out God! In the end, these refusals to commit amount to "idling" on the road of faith.

The Consequences of Noncommitment

What if young adults do not make commitments along the spiritual journey? What occurs if we do not choose to step forward on a chosen path? We run the risk of two alternatives, both not too hot for the spiritual life. The first is to allow life to lead us. This amounts to letting the car drift out of the garage, down the driveway, and out into the street in whatever direction happens to be downhill. The woman with the five jobs in a year might fit into this category. The other alternative is, of course, to stay where I am. On the spiritual journeys of life, one can easily choose to remain static. Maybe I stay in a stagnant dating relationship because it provides me with security. Or perhaps I keep going to church but I don't allow my faith to challenge me in any way. The static choice is easy, but it is usually a recipe for complacence or downright boredom. There is no place for either in the search for a mature faith.

We could talk more about the negative consequences of not committing, but it probably makes more sense to talk about the positive consequences of commitment. If any of us were to mentally click off the people we admire, I would hazard a guess that they are all people who have made commitments in their lives. The happy couples, the devoted parents, the competent scientists and engineers, the brilliant poets and painters—all these people have had to commit themselves to their pursuits, whatever they may be. That commitment means sweat and tears, yes, but it also means expertise and achievement in the long run. It means looking back with satisfaction. It means failure and disappointment at times, but it also provides the contentment of knowing that I stood for something in my life, that something was important enough to occupy a significant amount of my attention and time on this earth. In short, it is commitment that gives our lives richness and peace, challenges and growth. It cures both the restlessness of drifting and the depression of stagnating. It tests and develops our faith.

Spirituality and Commitment

Spiritual Faux Pas: Concluding that spirituality is a passivity that requires no commitment to anything or anyone.

To draw things together, we might remark that commitment is the way we say "yes" to God when God reaches out to us through events and people in our lives. God reaches out in an opportunity for friendship, through an urge to pray more regularly, or in the opportunity to promote social justice. Our response is to make a choice, to commit to what we believe the Spirit is calling us to. Yes, God's will is elusive at times, and we can never really be certain that we follow the Spirit's guidance with complete accuracy. But God does not expect perfection, only we do (more on this later).

Though the need for commitment on the road of faith may seem obvious at this point, we must confront the fact that there are those on the "spiritual scene" today who still argue with it. Some of the "gurus" ask us, "Isn't it more authentically spiritual to allow fate to take us where it will?" Thus, we strike upon the notion that true spirituality is passive, that choices, commitments, and decisions to accept certain lifestyles and traditions are bombs of artificiality that destroy the bunker of real spirituality. We should just sit back, and see what develops. The spiritual seeker should be that idling car drifting through the streets.

There is an appeal to this kind of spirituality. Commitment requires much from us, especially responsibility. In my quest to avoid this responsibility, I may desire to give all the responsibility to God and to abdicate my own opportunities to shape what happens in my life. In effect, I avoid making decisions so that I will not be responsible for what happens as a result. I charge God with that responsibility and let the road take me where it will. I give up my own freedom to choose, and I image God as either a controlling parent who must do everything for me or as a curious gambler who rolls the dice of human life over and over again in the hope that interesting combinations will appear. Neither of these encompasses the God who loves us, who desires to enter into relationship with us, the God of the Scriptures. That God respects our freedom and seeks to engage us as co-creators in the world we inhabit. That God enlists our assistance in transforming the world into the kingdom of God.

This passive spirituality is not a true spirituality. The proponents of this spirituality refuse to respond to the signs of the Holy Spirit at work in our world. This spirituality refuses to recognize our human dignity as free beings, created so by the God who wishes to enter into relationship with us. By making choices and commitments, on the other hand, we celebrate the dignity that is God's gift to us. Commitment, then, is praise for the Creator of our freedom!

Temporary Commitments

We speak of the need for commitment on our road of faith, but it bears remembering that not all commitment is permanent. Many of us feel that we are not yet fully prepared to make permanent commitments. We are not ready for marriage, for long-term career choices, for decisions to remain in one place for many decades to come. This is not a fear of commitment so much as an awareness of the limitations of our place in life. It is wisdom, not fear, that teaches us our limitations.

Yet commitment *is* important for the spiritual life. Clearly, then, a spirituality for young adults must include provisions for temporary commitments: I commit to a job for a year or two to test the waters; I move to a new town and decide to stay there for a period of two years to see if I like the area; and dating becomes essentially a practice of engaging in limited commitments. Eventually some of these temporary commitments lead to long-term or permanent commitments. It often happens that two people in the limited relationship of dating grow into a more exclusive relationship that leads to a permanent commitment. If the two people involved are truly mature and responsible enough to make that promise to each other, then it's time to rejoice and celebrate their commitment! If they are not yet ready, there is no hurry. Temporary commitments can do much to teach us about life and to prepare us for the few permanent commitments each of us makes in the course of a lifetime.

Enough said. We now move on to a more in-depth look at the sources of young adult avoidance of commitment. What gives us the relational cold feet, the vocational jitters, the occasional desire to outright turn and run? Is there a simple cause with a direct solution? We all know the answer to that; life seldom works that way. More likely, there are countless factors that go into a fear of commitment. In the following pages, we'll unpack a few of the possibilities in the hope of shedding some light on these hesitancies and fears. My hope here is that at least one of the following five angles on the fear of commitment will resonate with your experience.

Experience Addiction

Only the most depressed among us doubts that our road of faith is an exciting and stimulating place. The twists and turns, the different people and events, fill our lives with challenge and fun. God wills that we enjoy life! Yet this excitement can become an end in itself. We can, at times, become so entranced by the varied experiences possible that we focus chiefly on increasing them. We can become, in a manner of speaking, addicted. The situation ends up like that of someone entering the largest frozen yogurt shop in the world and becoming obsessed with sampling all the flavors. The problem (other than getting sick) is that this connoisseur never sits down to enjoy his yogurt! Exploring side roads is a wonderful diversion at times, but if it becomes the norm for our journey, then we never really get anywhere.

This endless sampling is an obstacle to commitment for many young adults. Recall the woman mentioned earlier who held several jobs in the course of one year. Think also of a college student you may know who changed his or her major six or seven times. Picture those times in your life when you had to try out everything and experience as much as you could. These are all variations on "flitting," wandering from interesting path to interesting path without making a commitment to any of them. We all do it from time to time. Some of it is an interesting and temporary distraction in life, an exploration of the variety in the universe. Yet too much of it bars us from any true success in life. Because I try six different religions (jobs, hobbies, clubs, etc.), I never become good at any of them. In fact, I may never get to know any of them well enough to know if I even like one of them.

Why do we run after experience like this? The answer lies in the nature of contemporary life. Our modern society provides far more stimuli than we can comprehend. Whereas our ancestors had only a few choices in their lives, we (those of us middle class and above, that is) have endless possibilities for experience, hundreds of different ways of learning, miles and miles of forests and towns down innumerable "side streets of faith." With this incredible panoply of experience competing for our attention, we develop understandable delusions of grandeur. We want to go for the gusto, to experience as much as we can before we have to settle down. In effect, many of us are addicted to experience, whether it be the experience of different cities, different jobs, different styles of prayer, or even different lovers. Experience becomes the overwhelming motivating factor in our lives. When there are no unusual or exciting experiences going on in our lives, we become bored and listless. We need that shot of experience to pump us back up for the journey of life.

This "experience addiction," like any addiction, teaches us a way of looking at life that is a lie. We know that alcoholism creates in the drinker the illusion that he or she is always in control. Overeating makes a person believe that food will bring happiness in unhappy situations (though it doesn't). Experience addiction has us buying into the idea that life is one big rush. Life ought to always be producing adrenaline in us, keeping us excited and full of energy. How true is this? Life can be exciting, but it can also be tedious. Some activities bring us instant rewards, whereas other life engagements reward us not in the short term but in the long term. Work, marriage, and faith are all of the latter category. These commitments give meaning to our lives and fulfill us through the long haul, but they do not always bring us immediate happiness and gratification.

If our journey requires us to stick to some of the roads we travel, could not repetition, the enemy of the experience addict, actually be a virtue? There are, in fact, spiritual lessons to be learned from repetition. It is the key to ritual. At Sunday mass or service, we repeat symbolic words and actions over and over again in worship. In the process, they take on a deeper-than-words significance. They begin to have a power that ordinary words and actions do not possess. Repetition also teaches us the importance of detail, the significance of little things. As human beings, we have the capacity not only to appreciate the majestic beauty of a great forest but also to celebrate the simplest leaf. Yet how many times is such a leaf repeated in the course of a forest? Finally, and along the same lines, repetition allows us to slow down and appreciate life.

Take eating, for example. Few activities could be more repetitive. Many of us (I am a prime offender) shovel our food down when we could be savoring each morsel! In any case, repetition is a part of the spiritual journey. It is not always a virtue (one would not want to hear the same sermon every Sunday), but it certainly can be.

Fear of Missing Out

The fear of missing out can also lead us to flit from experience to experience without commitment. Like experience addiction, it is a product of the astounding barrage of stimuli and choices we face in the contemporary world. Empowered with the knowledge of so many possibilities, some of us develop a real fear that the best opportunities in life may pass us by unless we are exceedingly vigilant. So we investigate each and every opportunity we encounter to ensure it isn't "the big one that got away."

"If I decide to stay with this job for two or three years more," a man muses to himself, "I will miss out on other career opportunities." So he tries a different job every four months! Sooner or later he will have to confront the truth— *we never get good at anything if we are trying everything.* Success along the road of faith requires that we make choices. With the possibilities many of us have, the situation is like that of the helicopter pilot who accidentally drops a wad of dollar bills while flying over a forest. The pilot can land and attempt a search of the entire area, or can scour through the most likely spots. He or she will probably collect more money the second way.

We are better off to narrow down our choices and commit ourselves in those areas we think are most likely to further us along the road of faith. Suppose I am a college freshman discerning the best major to pursue. If my passion is really for science, I do not waste my time exploring each and every field of study in the liberal arts. I might try a few, since new experiences help round out my perspective, but I will concentrate on investigating the sciences. This is an obvious example, but there are others that demonstrate the point. Suppose I feel the need for more personal prayer time in my life but am unsure about how to pursue that. Do I start to go through each book in the parish library that's on prayer? Rather I will probably ask someone whose spirituality I respect to recommend something.

Fear of missing out is all about avoiding lost opportunities, yet there is no way to avoid them. Making choices means other choices disappear from my life. If I move away from family and friends, I initially try to keep in touch with all of them. Eventually, however, as I develop friendships in the place I land, I will lose touch with some of these friends. And so it goes. Life means missed opportunities as well as gained ones. Sacrifices are a necessary part of every spiritual journey. Sometimes the sacrifices are not difficult. After people have been away from each other for a long time, they tend to drift apart so that the loss is not so intense. At other times, however, the choices are painful. To break off an engagement because of conflicting career or family goals may be for the best in the end, but it has painful consequences for the present.

We have to learn to mourn our lost opportunities, to feel the disappointment that we cannot be everything we want to be. It will not help to try to pretend that the lost opportunity meant nothing ("I really didn't want that job") or to ignore the feelings ("I'm tough and can handle this"). Instead, we are called to be compassionate with ourselves and accept the disappointment that choosing between two goods often brings. And we learn to trust God. If we cooperate with God in this process of discernment (to be discussed a few chapters later), we need not worry about every missed opportunity. God does not abandon us to make it on our own. God helps to guide us as we make our choices.

Is God Asking Too Much?

We have been looking at the reasons that young adults entertain too many options and thus are prevented from committing to a few. There is, however, another reason to avoid commitment. This one is more properly labeled as a fear. We speak of that piece of baggage known as the Fear of Getting in Over My Head. That duffel bag contains two giant wads of stress and a pocketful of worry. Some of us young adults are reluctant to commit because we fear burdens that we cannot handle. Anxious over that possibility, we refuse commitments and underinvest ourselves in the commitments we do make.

When examining this anxiety from the perspective of faith, we ask ourselves if God is asking too much of us. We speculate that God wishes to test us, to evoke our dependency by descending us into chaos; however, the real issue here is not our conception of God at all. Rather, it is a couple of other things—frustration at the countless aspects of our lives that are out of our control and lack of self-confidence. As for the first, let's face it, when we commit to something, we really do not know what will appear down the pike. Commitments are leaps of faith. When I take responsibility for the volunteers staying the night at a local homeless shelter, I assume that the scheduled folks will show up. Still, they may not do so. It is out of my control, and that is frustrating because I am nevertheless responsible! Given that, would it not be better if I did not commit to the responsibility at all? Seemingly, yes. But what if no one took on the responsibility at all? Life is risky. Better to face the uncertainties of commitments and deal with problems on a day-to-day basis. In addition, help is usually available should problems arise. After all, accepting help is a sign of wisdom and personal strength rather than weakness. Whatever occurs, the important thing here is to engage life! Engaging life requires commitment.

The other side of this fear of getting more than we can handle is the belief that we really cannot handle much. A great number of us lack self-confidence. How do we overcome this? Support and practice. We seek people in our lives who lift us up rather than tear us down, who encourage us rather than discourage us. And we practice. We try to get involved in a variety of things and to become proficient in a few. Over time (self-confidence does not arrive overnight), in our various commitments, we see what we can do, we try out things, stretch ourselves. Life informs us of our strengths and weaknesses. Self-confidence is not a cheap commodity, for there will always be failure and disappointment on the way to it. Yet if we trust that in love, God has created each of us as a being of infinite value and personal worth, we know that each of us has talents and strengths for this life.

Now, there is such a thing as overextending oneself. Moreover, keeping busy can be a way of shielding ourselves from the bigger issues of life. The key to a healthy journey toward mature faith is to travel at a speed we can safely manage, to choose our roads carefully, to turn back when we have to, and to keep aware as we drive along. Balance is called for. We learn over time to gauge when to say yes, when to say no, and when to wait and see.

Perfectionism

"Anything worth doing is worth doing badly." This piece of wisdom from my mother stomps on my personal favorite of all the reasons we avoid commitment—perfectionism. Many of us were somehow endowed with the expectation that we should always perform perfectly. Perhaps some authority figure taught us that we could only receive approval and affirmation if we did everything exactly right. Maybe we have started to believe the images of the media—bodies without fat or blemish, clothes always in style, heroes and heroines who always know how to respond to crisis. Or it could be that we have internalized the notion, embedded in American culture, that the successful person is always in control. However we developed this stressful expectation of perfection, it tends to infect our whole lives. We begin to count on perfection in all that we do. When we come up short (about ninety percent of the time), we either fall into depression or half-consciously cover up the mistake. We also start to expect flawless behavior from the people around us, and this leads to chronic disappointment when we find others to be merely human.

Perfectionism is so contagious that eventually it attacks our ability to commit ourselves. Looking at the different options put before us, we seek the perfect one—the perfect job, the perfect friend, the perfect major. How many of us spend our entire young adulthood looking for the perfect romance, for Mr. or Ms. Right. We reason that only those people that meet our inflated standards are worth our time and energy. But human beings are never perfect. We never find that perfect someone or job or whatever to make our life complete. We wander through life unwilling to commit ourselves in this imperfect world. Or we project the perfection we want on people and things that cannot measure up. The first time they disappoint us, we find our way to the exit door. Either way, our thirst for perfection keeps us from growing in faith.

In truth, perfectionism may work as a defense mechanism for us. Our incomplete sense of self-worth passionately fears failure, so we develop perfect standards and avoid commitment to anything that might end in failure. This defense does protect us from failure, but it also protects us from engaging life! It is the automatic garage door opener locked in the closed position. To get beyond that door, we have to face the possibility of failure.

Failure is a pervasive part of life, and no one can change that. In our lives, our generation of young adults will face failed careers, bankruptcies, divorces, bad health. Some of these we can head off, but others will catch us by surprise. On top of all this, we will face failure in our relationship with God, namely *sin*. We can try to pretend our way out of this, we can deceptively redefine our failures as successes, or we can look at reality and accept this darker side of human weakness. Accepting our failures brings us back to humility before the real Perfect One, our God on whom we depend.

From Problem to Solution: Dealing with Fear

How do we deal with our avoidance and fear of commitment? Once we know that we have a problem here, where do we look for a solution? Is there a psychological road crew we can call to fill in this pothole?

The first step is taking note of the reasons for our avoidance. If I avoid commitment because I am addicted to experience, I need to look at that and understand it in order to deal with it. If the cause is a type of emotional fear, I need to be aware of that. Whatever the reason (and there are many reasons untouched in this account), recognition begins the movement toward an ability to commit.

For many of us, our avoidance of commitment is based on some type of emotional fear. If we are not afraid of missing out or of failure, then we are frightened, for example, of being hurt in a committed relationship. To understand these fears better, we can classify them. Some of them are rational fears. These fears are a part of our reactions to practical situations in the here and now. Usually a combination of awareness and realism enables us to deal with them. A New Yorker in rural

Montana may retain the urban fear of walking the streets at night alone, but once he identifies this fear and assesses the chances of actually being mugged in rural Montana, his fear will vanish. He discovers that his fear is no longer reasonable. On the other hand, if he moves to Los Angeles, the fear is probably reasonable. In this case, he cannot simply dismiss the fear, but he can take appropriate precautions (do errands in the daytime, use his car at night) so that his fear does not dominate his life. Our mobile New Yorker aside, these lessons about rational fears apply to our fear of commitment. Once we understand what is going on, we can often discard our fear or at least keep it from dominating our life. No one would dispute that a fear of getting hurt in relationships is a rational response; none of us escapes this kind of hurt. But most of us also realize that to allow such a fear to prevent us from seeking friends and companions does not make sense. So we acknowledge the fear, say a hopeful prayer, and move on.

Some fears, of course, aren't so easily dispensed with. Irrational fears are a different matter and are more difficult to eliminate from our lives. A young person may understand rationally that his chances of being mugged are slim to none but retain the fear nonetheless, perhaps because of some previous traumatic experience of assault. This is an irrational fear, unresponsive to knowledge. Such fears are more difficult to handle and usually require a healing process over time. Everyone has them, including us men, who hate to admit it. Unfortunately, most of the fears that chase us from our commitments are of this variety. The fear of "getting in over my head" is usually rooted in an exaggerated fear of the loss of control. This could be brought on by a number of life experiences, but it does not pass away easily. Another irrational fear is that God will give me more than I can handle. After all, we believe in an all-loving God, not a God who enjoys torturing us. Again, this often actually revolves around anxiety over loss of control in life. The important thing is to accept that irrational fears are a part of the human condition. Rather than judge ourselves or others for them or fixate on them, we need to learn to deal with them.

Dealing with irrational fear generally means committing oneself to a long-term healing process while at the same time negotiating short-term strategies for bypassing the fear. We speak of "dealing with fear" here rather than eliminating it, because many of these fears will only disappear over a long period of time; and some of them may never disappear. Thus, we cannot pretend that an expert—psychologist, guru, spiritual director, or self-help writer—can make them instantly go away. Nor can we avoid or escape them. Instead, we recognize them. Next, we try to "meet" the fear, to get to know it, understand it, massage it a bit, allow it to exist without a judgment. Like any emotion, fear must be accepted and not repressed! The final step is to keep it out of the picture as much as we can when making choices. Decisions made out of fear usually paralyze us and keep us from moving on. Decisions that stretch beyond our fears put us in the arena of *risk*, the place where growth and challenge happen. This brings us to our final theme for this chapter.

Beyond Fear of Commitment: Guts, Help, and Grace

> Then the Lord said [to Moses], "I have observed the misery of my people who are in Egypt; I have heard their cry on account of their taskmasters. Indeed, I know their sufferings, and I have come down to deliver them from the Egyptians....So come, I will send you to Pharaoh to bring my people, the Israelites, out of Egypt." But Moses said to God, "Who am I that I should bring the Israelites out of Egypt?" God said, "I will be with you...." But Moses said to God, "If I come to the Israelites and say to them, 'The God of your ancestors has sent me to you,' and they ask me, 'What is his name?' what shall I say to them?" God said to Moses, "I AM WHO AM....Thus you shall say to the Israelites, 'I AM has sent me to you.'"

> But Moses said to the Lord, "O my Lord, I have never been elo-
> quent, neither in the past nor even now that you have spoken
> to your servant; but I am slow of speech and slow of
> tongue....O my Lord, please send someone else." Then the
> anger of the Lord was kindled against Moses and he said,
> "What of your brother Aaron, the Levite? I know that he can
> speak fluently....You shall speak to him and put the words in his
> mouth; and I will be with your mouth and with his mouth, and
> will teach you what you shall do...." Moses went back to his
> father-in-law Jethro and said to him, "Please let me go back to
> my kindred in Egypt and see whether they are still living." And
> Jethro said to Moses, "Go in peace." (Ex 3:7–14, 4:10–18)

As it was for Moses, there are those times in our lives when
fear of commitment is before us. We recognize it, we understand it, and we know we have to move on anyway. In these
situations, how do we keep our fear of commitment at bay as
we make choices for ourselves? How do we manage to keep
our eyes on the road when we hit this glorious pothole? We
need a generous supply of two things—guts and grace.

Many potholes resist repair, as those of us living in colder
climates know too well. In the same way, some fears will not
be dispelled by naming them or thinking them through or
even by understanding whence they come. We have to make
a disciplined effort to move on despite them. I may not feel
like moving another inch down my chosen road, but there are
times when I just have to put the damn car in gear and do it.
I move in spite of my fear instead of because of it. Nine times
out of ten I can use the adrenaline created by my fear to get
past it! In essence, what we are talking about here is a leap
of faith, a hurdling of the fear to continue the race on down
to the joys and challenges to come.

This sounds stoic, but it does not have to be so. I am not
called upon to keep my fears to myself. I am permitted to
complain about them out loud, just as Moses did to God. I
can cry while others comfort me. In fact, there are those
moments when we are so frightened that we need to take

someone else's hand before we make that leap of faith. For us today, the leap of faith of marriage is ritualized in our society so that we do not have to hurl ourselves headlong into it without support from others—family, close friends, clergy.

But even our valiant attempts at "hurdling" our fears and our essential human capacity to depend on one another does not complete the picture of overcoming fear. All Christians agree that our own efforts, even coupled with the assistance of our fellow travelers on the road of faith, are not enough to tackle the most difficult parts of the human journey. We are not perfect beings, and we need God. It is God who loved us into being; and if it were not for God's care at every moment, we would cease to exist! It is only through God's transforming power that we are able to get beyond some of our worst fears.

In other words, when we get stalled on the road of faith, when our fear of commitment keeps us from enjoying the richness and joy of life, God the Holy Spirit can be a kind of tow truck that either tows us on to the next rest stop or else gives us a jump start to get moving again on our own. These "tows" and "jump starts" can come in many colors, shapes, and sizes—through the encouragement or challenge of a friend or mentor, through a sudden change in perspective, through the interplay of circumstances, through the right words that somehow seem to come at the right time. Occasionally, we may even wake up one day to discover that the thing that frightened us most doesn't hold the same sway over us that it did!

There are any number of ways that the Spirit can help us to move beyond our fears. The trick is to be open, to be watching for that divine help in whatever form it may come. And it helps if we can put our trust in God. That is a tall order—after all, who can see God or know when God is going to act?—but it saves us a lot of anxiety. Without that trust, we are always worrying that the "tow truck" is never going to come. Trusting in the Lord, then, requires its own kind of leap of faith. Sometimes it takes guts to accept grace.[1] But not always. Sometimes, God the Spirit works in our lives despite us.

It's worth noting here that these three strategies for over-coming our fears—guts, depending on others, and depending on God—speak of who we are as human beings in a funda-mental way. We know that human beings are unique in that we have control over our destinies. We can set goals, over-come obstacles, and achieve these goals (some of the time, anyway). This is the courage piece of who we are. We also know that we are fundamentally beings in relationship with others—as friends, neighbors, family, members of society. We need each other throughout our lives. And we know that our relatedness extends beyond what we see. We believers rec-ognize that God's care, God's involvement in our lives, is another piece of the human puzzle. Grace is always around us. We are always on "holy ground."

III —

Chapter Four: SCAMS OF FAITH—
LOSING OUR SPIRITUAL MYTHS

In his famous spiritual myth, *The Great Gatsby,* F. Scott Fitzgerald's hero reinvents his identity. Hoping to win the heart of the beloved Daisy, through mysterious and morally dubious means, he makes himself into the careless, rich, superficial, and dashing man he believes Daisy desires. His self-transformation draws her in at first, but ultimately it fails. It becomes clear as well that Daisy cannot provide the spiritual fulfillment that the literally self-made man expects. Both his regeneration and his goal of winning Daisy are discovered to be "scams of faith," illusory ways to find meaning in life. Having fully bought into them, Gatsby is a lost and disoriented man at the end of the book.

In every age and for every group of people, there are spiritual myths. In his novel, Fitzgerald meant to expose some of those current to young Americans in the 1920s. These myths always look like they are going to be helpful to us, to take us places, to make our lives better. We buy into them, and for a while they may keep our lives afloat. But if we depend on them long enough, they break down on us, leaving us stranded on the road of faith. We end up dumping the myths in our own "spiritual junkyard," but only after many weeks, months, or even years of pain and hardship.

Sometimes we can avoid Gatsby's trap. Keeping alert and attentive to what goes on around us can deliver us from blindly buying into spiritual myths. For example, if we are aware of the tenor of conversation in a group, we will likely note when the talk dwells too much on the negative, perhaps before we have begun to fall into negativity ourselves! On the other hand, even attentiveness does not prevent us from digesting a few unhealthy myths. These are often unquestioned assumptions of our culture—the comfortable life that is necessary for happiness, the stoic independence that defines manhood, and so on. In a manner of speaking, they are part of the "religion" we have absorbed from our environment, the religion we need to lose. Many of these myths disproportionately affect young adults.

We humans are complex beings. We can be misled and misdirected without any awareness on our part. Thus, daily life calls for a healthy amount of skepticism. It is necessary to question even our most basic assumptions at times: Who sold me this idea? Have they misled me before? Is this helpful to myself or other people, or is it subtly hurtful? What does my gut tell me about this? Most young adults are familiar with this process; we learned it while beginning to question the values and answers of their parents. We may recognize it from the times when we have taken another look at our assumptions about gender roles. It is a part of the discernment of the Holy Spirit's workings in our lives, a topic that will occupy much of our attention later. For now, let us just say that all of us spend our lives discovering and repenting of unhealthy conceptions about reality. The key is to recognize these spiritual myths before they let us down. With God's help, we can sometimes catch ourselves before the hurt is too great.

Myth #1: There Are Spiritual Elevators

Spiritual Faux Pas: Opting for the spiritual elevator.

As we travel down the seedy boulevard, surveying the used car lots, we glimpse one of the biggest scams of all—the spiritual elevator. Press a button and the mysterious metal box lifts you to Wisdom and Inner Peace. Press another and you are on your way to Holiness. It sounds ridiculous, but the metaphor is precise. Most of us want wisdom right now, inner peace instantly, perfect love without working at it! We are in search of "microwave spirituality," "minute faith," and "instant peace" our fast-moving culture of convenience has taught us to expect.

But there is no "quik-spirituality"; there really are no spiritual elevators. In elevators, we take an easy ride; we don't talk to anyone along the way; we focus on our destination. But our spiritual journeys do not make for such short and tidy travelogues. Finding our mature faith requires years of commitment, prayer, and rapport with both peers and mentors. Spiritual growth moves in stages and phases in which our relationship with God changes and develops. Each time we believe we have finally found "the answers," another crisis appears and leads us to growth in a new area. The key ingredient to our spiritual journey is time. There is no overnight mail to God. We have to put in our years to find our faith.

Myth #2: Growing Up Is for Later

We've probably all indulged. We've opted to hide responsibility, commitment, work, and serious pursuits in the trunk of our spiritual vehicles so that they wouldn't get in the way of our having a good time. Who among us has not refused commitments we feared would tie us down? Who has not stayed out late having fun the night before a test at school or an important day at work? One myth we have purchased at the market of self-deception says to us, "You can grow up later."

Who sells us this doozy of a lie? I suppose its appearance is inevitable in a time of transition such as young adulthood. It is certainly an old and widespread myth. For years now, we have romanticized the young adult wanderer. And at some point or other, most of us young adults have resisted the responsibilities and commitments that come with adulthood. But what are the consequences of this myth? Well, "partying" the night before a day of work usually means an unproductive day at work. Shirking all responsibilities and commitments means at best that our resumés remain fairly empty in the accomplishment department. Maybe we let other people down that were counting on us.

Life is too short for growing up later. Maturation is a lifelong process of discovery and growth, and we cannot afford to begin it sometime well into our thirties or forties. The needs and problems of our world require energetic young people who are focused and mature. And it is not boring to be mature. Maturity also involves spontaneity and playfulness, a sense of fun and energy that recharges us and refuels us for the struggles of life. Part of being mature, as a friend of mine used to remark, is knowing when and where you can still be immature!

Myth #3: Heaven Can Wait (Spiritual Procrastination)

Spiritual Faux Pas: Thinking that spirituality, religion, and faith are matters suited to those who have "settled down," not to those who are young and "untethered."

A common myth of our culture asserts the importance of spirituality but says that we can delay dealing with spirituality until we are "established" in a job, marriage, and family. If this

rings true at all, then spirituality should actually be thought of
as one chapter in a book about family life rather than as the
lifelong story of faith. Faith, then, is not a life-giving commitment to God, but rather part of the institution of family. I take
up spirituality (like I would bridge or bowling?) because that
is what "settled" people do. Or perhaps I take up spirituality
with parenthood to give my children a moral foundation. But
isn't faith something more than a "preschool in morality"?

These notions of spirituality are not completely off base.
Faith *is* a part of family life, and it *does* teach children moral
values. But these are only pieces of the whole picture.
Spirituality concerns itself with our whole life journey, our
growth along the way, our relationships with other human
beings and with God. Thousands of years of collected human
wisdom witness to its relevance to everyone's life. To put spirituality in a box called "family life" is to compartmentalize
God!

What are the consequences of this spiritual procrastina-
tion? Does this attitude stall us on the road of faith? A friend
of mine observed that it is not so much an obstacle on the
road of faith as it is "idling in the garage." By relegating "spiritual matters" (actually, all matters are spiritual) to later in life,
we waste a lot of precious energy and time. We refuse to deal
with matters of our own growth, of the meaning of our lives.

In addition, a reluctance to approach spiritual issues in
younger days makes certain crisis moments more difficult
later on in life. Natural crises like the death of a close friend
or family member force us to focus on the serious spiritual
questions of life and death, and on what they both mean. If
we have not reflected on these matters before, we end up trying to deal with them using a child's spirituality and a child's
faith. We will either find ourselves in an emergency growth
session at a difficult time, or we will break down and be unable
to deal with the issues at all. On the other hand, by focusing
our attention on our spiritual journeys during young adult-

hood, we get on with the business of life and invite ourselves
to grow through the intervening grace of the Holy Spirit.

Myth #4: Immortality

Consider these startling statistics about the abuse of alcohol
on college campuses: 1) of those students who are currently
undergraduates, more will eventually die from alcohol-related
causes than will receive postgraduate degrees; 2) ninety percent of all campus rapes involve alcohol; 3) more money is
spent on alcohol each year than on books and all nonalcoholic
beverages combined; 4) ninety percent of all violent crime on
campus is alcohol-related; 5) alcohol is involved in twenty-
eight percent of those cases where students drop out of college.[1]

This is not to say that all young adults have a problem with
alcohol. Most do not. The point is that at times young adults
behave as if we were immortal, as if nothing could touch us.
We take unnecessary risks for immediate gratification. We do
not consider the possible ill effects in the long term. Some of
us drink excessively and yet believe ourselves immune to alcoholism. Others drive too fast or tailgate. (I myself have a dangerous habit of daydreaming at the wheel.) Still others rashly
attack their bosses and teachers without a rational plan of
confrontation. And, of course, there is the now famous but
still common practice of engaging in risky sexual behavior.
Meanwhile the number of unwanted pregnancies, abortions,
and AIDS cases among young adults remains high.

What is going on here? We are not stupid. Are we naive,
thinking that bad things don't happen to us? Can it be that
death and danger seem too remote to our experience to truly
be a threat? I remember when I worked on a roller coaster for
a summer job, the kids would ask me playfully, "Am I going to
die?" The answer that always came to me (and I confess once

or twice I said it) was, "Yes, eventually." This is how it is with most human beings. We know intellectually of our mortality and fragility, but sometimes it is difficult for that knowledge to penetrate our daily decision making. Yet we really need to dispense with our illusions of immortality and be aware of our limitations as embodied human beings. We need not shut ourselves inside and avoid the world, but we can conduct our lives with appropriate caution. We have to take risks, and sometimes we will be hurt because of them. That is learning. But we need not be reckless.

Myth #5: The Myth About Romantic Love

Spiritual Faux Pas: Believing that another person can be our happiness and our spiritual fulfillment.

"I need you." "I can't live without you." "All I want is you." "You're going to make me so happy." "My life had no meaning before you came." Uh-oh, danger.

Romantic love is a wonderful gift of God. It enriches and beautifies our lives. It awakens us to life when we remain emotionally dead. Falling in love is a basic and positive human experience. It places us in a unique and vulnerable position vis-à-vis another person. It puts a song in our hearts! And we can learn so much from it, if we are paying attention.

Unfortunately, often when we are in love, we are so carried away by the experience that we are not paying attention. The song in our hearts is on "endless loop." It drowns out all the other songs of life. Instead of enjoying an occasional respite from rationality (as we should), we take an indefinite vacation. We set ourselves adrift on a sea of emotion. Soon every fulfillment is linked to the beloved. She or he assumes the roles of Key to Our Happiness and General Motivator of Our Behavior.

As most of us have found at one time or another, this never

works. No one can find my fulfillment for me. No one can be my chauffeur down the road of faith while I sit back and wallow in my emotions. The object of my obsession cannot lead me to God; in fact, he or she becomes a kind of god to me. I must always please the person, must always be assured of his or her presence in my life, must avoid doing things to displease this person. I spend such effort and time on the relationship that I have no effort left for anything else—friends, work, spirituality. When the delights of falling in love turn into the life-consuming dependencies of obsession, I have made a wrong turn. This situation may even grow into a kind of addiction, and that can be a real conversation stopper in my relationship with God. As with alcoholism and drug abuse, love addiction must be dealt with before I can get on with my spiritual journey.[2]

Myth #6: Spirituality—Seeing Life as Black and White

Spiritual General's Warning: Black and white thinking has been shown to be harmful to a person's spiritual health.

There is a wonderful novel by humorist and writer Christopher Buckley called *Thank You for Smoking*. It deals with the adventures of a spokesman for the tobacco companies. The main character's job is to convince the public that smoking is not really bad for you. The reader cannot but be amused by the utterly ludicrous double-talk and manipulation. How does someone say all this with a straight face when the evidence is so clear?

This "spiritual myth" works in about the same way. Spirituality deals with reality as it is, as God has made it. God has made life a rich, varied, complicated experience. Anyone who has ever opened a biology textbook or tried to understand someone from another culture or discussed biomedical ethics knows that this is true. Throughout the centuries, however, human institutions—even religious institutions—have tried to get us to trust in their version of life, a version that is not complicated. We are asked to buy into a worldview that puts everything into simple categories. This despite the fact that the evidence for a more nuanced and complicated world is overwhelming! For example, for centuries, my own Roman Catholic Church taught that sex was bad and should be avoided except for purposes of procreation. Today, some fundamentalist groups (of various religions) insist that belonging to their group makes you good, whereas belonging to all others makes you bad. The ideas in both outlooks are simple, black and white. But is this reality? Is this what God created?

Black-and-white thinking is seductive. It offers security and simple, easily understood options. It relieves us of responsibility for our own views about life. We don't have to decipher reality on our own. We don't even have to reflect on our experience and that of other people. The answers are right there for us. And, we are told, they are certainly right. You see the problem. We have certainty again instead of faith. We have guarantees instead of trust. It's that old religion returning, refusing to be lost! We cannot afford this kind of thinking on our spiritual journeys. It leads us down smooth highways that take us nowhere, straight and easy thoroughfares that look clean and wholesome but lead us in circles.

Can we not see the complications and nuances of life as enhancing the spiritual journey, making it interesting and beautiful? It would be terrible if we woke up one day, realized that all religious truth is simply read in the Bible, and then decided that there was nothing more to learn in the realm of spirituality. What kind of a life would that be? There would be no more learning on the hard but satisfying road of personal experience. We would never again go through the excitement of struggling with a difficult question about who God is for us or what a passage of scripture means to people today. The road of faith would be always the same.

Who wants to take a trip down a road that looks exactly the same the whole way? We need twists and turns, multiple layers of scenery. We need surprises to keep us growing and changing. I know personally that if I accepted that reality was black and white, I would become complacent and bored with my life. I don't believe that is what God wants for us. God wants us to discover all the different colors, experiences, and nuances along the road of faith. We are invited to enjoy their richness and allow them to teach us about the Maker who created them.

Myth #7: "I Know What I'm Doing" and Other Guarantees

I hate backseat drivers. I admit it. Why? Backseat drivers question my ability to drive. They do not trust that I will keep them safe. On the other hand, I am a backseat driver. After all, I know that *I* can be trusted to drive safely and efficiently—but do *other* people really know how to drive? So I give advice, gasp, clutch the seat, and press down on the imaginary brake in front of me. What's going on here? I am trying to guarantee my own safety in a situation over which in actuality I have no control whatsoever.

It is perhaps that same desire for "guarantees" that leads me to react defensively to other backseat drivers. I could just evaluate the offending passenger's suggestion rationally. If he is right, I ought to change my habits. No big deal. But instead, I take it personally. I take the slightest criticism as a threat to my psychological security. After all, I know what I'm doing! This is my guarantee. If I didn't know what I was doing, my world would fall apart, wouldn't it?

But there are no guarantees, and we don't have to be afraid of this. As Jesus says in the Gospels, "Fear is useless; what is needed is trust" (Mk 5:36). A realistic view admits that there are no guarantees in life. Things will not always go my way. I will not always know what I am doing. Our fear calls us to rely on our own sense of control, but the Holy Spirit calls us to rely on God. After all, our guarantees may be taken away. We are better off if we base our psychological security on the fact that we are loved by God and that God never forgets us.

This is difficult, of course. To rely on God in this way is faith; and faith, as we know, is not the same thing as certainty. Faith is a leap, not a guarantee. It involves doubts and questions. It must in order to grow. It will be a struggle from the day we come of age to the day we die. But it is a good struggle, a worthy struggle, and it has its rewards. God can be trusted, after all. Unfortunately, it is all too easy to abandon that trust in God and put it in something that human beings have made.

Myth #8: Life Is to Be Analyzed and Worried About

After hearing about the misleading myths that permeate our young adult subculture, a person could get the idea that life is so dangerous and subtly diabolical that we can never let down our guard. If you are neurotic like I am, this is food for anxiety and endless analysis about every moment of life. Others may find themselves overly skeptical or cynical about life in our culture. Neither attitude is warranted. Within these pages, I mean to suggest a few of the spiritual pitfalls of young adulthood that have appeared in my experience and in that of some other young adults. They are merely a few things that you may find helpful. I hope they will not drive anyone to anxiety. God did not give us life so that we might worry and analyze our way through each moment. Life is to be lived! Carpe diem!

‖≡

Chapter Five: BALANCING OUR BURDENS

> At that time Jesus said, "Come to me, all you that are weary and are carrying heavy burdens, and I will give you rest. Take my yoke upon you, and learn from me; for I am gentle and humble in heart, and you will find rest for your souls. For my yoke is easy, and my burden is light." (Mt 11:28–29)

Driving down the interstate, you have probably seen those weigh stations where state police officers inspect and weigh trucks to ensure that they are under the legal highway limit. I've often wondered if there ought to be "spiritual weigh stations," where we could weigh our spiritual and emotional baggage. Then, at least, there would be a way of *knowing* whether we carry too much of it.

We all carry extra baggage in our lives. Different times in our lives spell different kinds of burdens. Part of the spiritual life is recognizing and balancing these burdens. Our faith is designed to set us free, not to weigh us down. As we grow in faith, it becomes easier to discard and manage the thousand burdens of life. The burden of Jesus is light; we pray the Holy Spirit to come into our lives, relieve us of the burdens we have chosen and those we have inherited, and give us the freedom of the yoke of Jesus the Christ.

Parental Expectations

Most famous among young adult burdens is that of parental expectations. The size of this burden varies from young adult to young adult. For some of us, it is a modest wad. Others of us have to rent a U-Haul trailer to drag it around! It is the difference between those who worry about whether their mothers approve of the language they use and those who feel their careers must proceed according to the expectations generated by their parents.

Though the "heaviness" of parental expectations differs, it plays some kind of role in the spiritual journey of each of us as young adults. Even when our parents do not tell us what to do, we can still feel their influence in a number of subtle ways. Some of us have an internalized voice that reminds us of our parents' wishes for us. At the department store cashier, clothing purchase in hand, a voice from inside wonders, "Would Mom like this?" Others of us hear an inner voice not consciously connected with our parents, but one that nonetheless is always judging, approving, or disapproving, probably connected with God or some authority figure. This is what Freud called the *superego,* and it finds its origins in parental expectations. For example, faced with choosing a major in college, I know that I "just have to major in business," though I am not entirely sure why.

Finally, there are those of us who make a half-conscious turnabout, who have an irrational desire to do exactly the *opposite* of what our parents would want. If my parents value education, I quit school. If they want me to vote Democrat, I vote Republican. We rebel, hoping in this manner to triumph over parental control. But rebellion is just another way to live our lives reacting to our parents' expectations. Rebellion does not, in reality, mean independence.

Why do we call parental influence a "burden"? Doesn't the voice of a parent in our head give us the right answer now and then? Suppose my parents' disapproval prevents me from joining a cult. Don't our parents sometimes have our best interests at heart? Don't they have significant life experience by which we can learn? Obviously, the answers to these questions can be "yes." Still, parental expectations can be and usually are a burden. Part of the process of growing in maturity along the road of faith is developing a sense of my own personal authority. When I am faced with the decision of what church to attend, mature faith means *I* decide. I may take my parents' preference (and possible wisdom) into account, but *I* choose. Yet children are not capable of making their own decisions on many issues, so they depend on the authority of adults. As we grow into adults, more and more authority is granted us. But it takes a while for our psychological selves to catch up, and thus, we young adults find ourselves wading through the expectations of parents and authority figures trying to find our own voices.

Though difficult at times, finding one's inner voice is a wonderful journey of self-discovery. Unfortunately, this process of self-discovery gets short-circuited when we are so absorbed in dealing with our parents' expectations (whether by obeying them, worrying about them, or rebelling against them) that we have no energy left to try to understand who we are. It's as if our parents have formed a box for us, and we choose to live in it. Boxes get in the way of reality. The spiritual journey, on the other hand, concerns itself with what is real, with discovering the reality of God truly active in the world around me and within me.

How then do we deal with this box? The solution is not to blame my parents. Blame is absolutely useless. I am responsible for my own destiny, not them. If my parents have too much control over my life, it is because I allow it. We should never forget the old Hindu proverb that the one who points the finger at someone else is also pointing his other three fingers back at himself! Blaming our parents can be something of a national sport for young adults. We all go through stages of holding our parents responsible for every bad habit and neurosis we have. But blame shifts the responsibility away from me; and furthermore, it implies unresolved anger and resentment, signs that the burden of parental expectations is weighted down with emotional baggage. This baggage is *my* responsibility.

Unloading the burden of our parents' expectations can be a long and difficult process, and it often requires the help of supportive friends and a counselor or spiritual director. With supportive friends, we might share the difficulties of trying to overcome what our parents want of us. Each of us needs to share with those who know from experience the shame of "never quite measuring up," the confusion of not knowing the difference between what I want and what others want, the self-directed anger of not having made decisions for myself. We will also need the input of an older adult, a companion on the road who knows the way beyond the burden of parental expectations. We benefit greatly from someone who is not in any way a parent to us, but who has already navigated these waters and landed safely and sanely on the other side.

When we begin to unload the burden of living by our parents' expectations, we taste the freedom of independence and interdependence. We dream new dreams for ourselves and discover our own expectations. We relate to our parents as adults, taking their advice as legitimate input, secure in the knowledge that we make our own decisions and that we may choose to follow their advice or not. Perhaps we have advice for them! And they too have the right to refuse it.

Peers' Expectations

Lest our parents seem like villains, the expectations of others also bear mention. The term *peer pressure* is more associated with teenagers than with young adults (and has become a cliché as well), and yet the weighty expectations of our peers can be a burden on the road of faith. Our peers have ideas about what types of jobs we ought to have, where we ought to live, how we should dress, and how we should spend our time and money. Sometimes these expectations are based on their needs and desires and not ours. Friends may call on us to "party" more often so that they can justify their own drinking habits. People have ulterior motives. (This is a fact about human beings, not a blanket judgment on all young adults.)

Certainly our peers seldom plot our spiritual downfall or willfully mislead and hurt us. Nevertheless, their expectations of us (often unconscious) are not always founded in concern for our good. They may be. They may expect us to exercise, eat well, and have quality relationships. These would be helpful expectations. Or they might want us to assist them in verbally ripping a neighbor to shreds. The expectations themselves, of course, are not the problem. The problem comes when we approach expectations uncritically, when we blindly do what people require of us. As in the case of our parents' expectations, blind obedience to, or a blanket rebellion against, the desires of our peers does not lead to a mature spirituality. Mature people do not remain paralyzed by the expectations of others. They may feel the pull of others' feelings, but they make their own decisions.

The Expectations of Culture and Church

Several years ago two friends were married. As they prepared for the event, they had to confront the question of having children. The truth is, neither of them felt particularly inclined toward parenthood. It was not that they feared commitment. Both are devoted high school teachers who see this as their vocation, their calling in life. Rather, when they searched their hearts and thought it all out, consulted friends and mentors, and prayed, they became convinced that they were not called to be parents. As the years progressed, they held to this belief; however, they were unprepared for the flack they received from all kinds of people in their lives. Their families berated them; many friends looked at them as if they were insane when they heard the story. Behind their backs, people talked about how selfish they were. Even worse was the reaction among their fellow churchgoers who considered it unchristian and certainly against Catholic principles not to have children.

In our era of individualism, we are often blind to the burdensome expectations of culture and church. These are perhaps even more difficult to thwart than the expectations of parents or peers. When we go against the prevailing expectations of culture or church (as my friends did), people react with fear. It is seen as a direct challenge to our collective way of life. Ask anyone who espouses virginity at the university dorms or who tries to remain a faithful churchgoer after coming out as gay or lesbian. Question a Catholic seminarian about the leper-like treatment he receives over the issue of celibacy. It is hard work to buck the system, even if I believe in my heart of hearts that I do so in good faith with good reason.

Deep-seated taboos and unconscious fears keep cultural expectations in place. We struggle with these throughout our lives, but it is particularly hard for young adults, for our ego strength is tentative, just beginning to grow. But the struggle remains important if we are to grow into "spiritual adults."

Naiveté

As we grow, so does the psychological baggage that we carry on the road of faith. Experience hands us new fears and resentments, grudges and long angers. Accordingly, young adulthood is a time generally marked by more enthusiasm and positive energy than later adulthood. We are more earnest, more eager for life, less marked by the things that slow us down. But the dark side of this is naiveté. Experience bestows baggage, but it also bestows lessons and fills in blind spots. We may be free of much of the weight of experience, but we carry the impressive heft of inexperience. This allows us to be deceived, opens us up for betrayal, gets us hurt. We have to constantly pull over and readjust our load, throwing off a portion of the load of naiveté each time we get hurt and thereby make a discovery.

I have an acquaintance who was in a long and destructive romantic relationship. She was deeply in love, and she was naive to the idea that a person would manipulate her in the context of a love affair. Unfortunately, that is precisely what happened. He capitalized on her fears and desires in order to control her, forcing her into emotional games, always getting his way. She had little experience in love and could not see what was happening. The relationship was tearing her apart, dragging her down on her life journey. Finally, after many impassioned pleas on the part of parents and friends, she opened her eyes, dumped her burden of naiveté (and him), and got on with the business of life.

We have to watch and listen. When we are attentive to our own behaviors and those of others, really stepping outside of ourselves to reflect and analyze, we can sometimes read the signs of the times and prevent a disaster. When we listen to the comments of friends, parents, and wisdom figures in our lives, we may discover pitfalls we could not recognize from our own point of view.

A healthy sense of skepticism will serve us as well. The world is not out to get us, but neither is it necessarily out for our good. We must also be prepared to crash and burn. Not perfect beings, we are not always going to "see it coming."

Hurt, betrayal, deception—these things are painful, but they have much to teach us. They can strengthen us. There are lessons learned only by direct experience. There are strengths only gained when scars replace the wounds. To engage ourselves in life means to risk pain and suffering, but we survive and grow stronger!

The Insecurity of "Who Am I?"

Much energy is spent by young adults in answering the question "Who am I?" We deal with questions and decisions of education, companionship, vocation, community involvement, how to spend our free time. This is appropriate! Older adults evaluate their life experiences. Middle-aged adults consider their work and relationships. Children discover their surroundings. We wrestle with our place in the world. Our spiritual and developmental task is to discover and shape the divinely imaged individual in each of us.

Naturally, this task requires a substantial part of our energy and focus. It is both burdensome and exciting! Older adults, who have a stronger sense of themselves, focus more exclusively on the spiritual issues of serving God and the community through their particular vocation and life. Think of the movie *Parenthood,* where Steve Martin and Mary Elizabeth Mastrantonio spend nearly every moment of their day either caring for their children or worrying about caring for them, stealing moments here and there for intimacy between them! As comically so for those two, the burden in this stage of life is the plethora of outside expectations. Young adults, on the other hand, begin to confront these issues while simultaneously devoting the largest part of our energy to self-discovery. As a result, we sometimes shortchange our external commitments and are accused of being self-centered and self-

absorbed—the "me generation." The accusation is often
unfair. The balancing act is not easy.

How do we do it? How do we answer the query of "Who
am I"? Maybe we get to know ourselves the same way we
come to know others. We commit time to the relationship.
We spend time alone. A friend of mine recently ended a two-
year stint of living alone. She found it liberating in a specific
way. She had spent so many years acting on the wishes of others that she did not know what she herself wanted out of life.
As she spent more time alone, she began to ask herself questions and to actively listen for the internal responses. She
began to monitor her own behavior and try to read what it
told her. She treated herself well, determined to demonstrate
a healthy self-regard. For my friend, these were some of the
building blocks of self-discovery.

Self-knowledge, however, does not come only in solitude,
important as that is. We probably learn more about ourselves
in relationships than we do on our own. How do certain
people affect us and why? How do our life experiences
affect the way we relate to older people, to children, to the
opposite sex? We can listen for our interior responses as we
relate to others. We can reflect back on our behavior toward
friends, co-workers, and family and try to understand what
occurs. And, after all, doesn't the best of our self-reflection
happen when we share with an intimate friend? So often I
learn about me by listening to the experience of someone in
a similar situation. As for demonstrating self-regard, we often
do so by spending time with the people we enjoy most.

Leaping into a Phone Booth: Transitions in Young Adulthood

In nonindustrialized societies, anthropologists tell us, there
are distinct ritualized plans for every major transition in life.

When a young woman begins her menstrual periods, she is isolated among the womenfolk for a specified time. When a young man becomes a warrior, he must spend a significant period in the wilderness alone. Whether a person is tackling adulthood, marriage, parenthood, or a position of leadership, the transition is well marked. It is also universally respected. Everyone must treat the person differently once the ritual is complete. It's almost as if a person jumps into a phone booth (à la Superman) in one life state and emerges again fully transformed into another.

In our own postindustrialized society, these rituals and traditions have largely disappeared. Even the last vestiges of such rituals—*quinciñieras,* going-away parties, college graduations—do not assume the significance they used to. We are no longer certain about when transitions take place. Many couples live together before marriage. Only after several months or years do college graduates adjust to being in the workforce full-time. There are no more phone booths, though we long for them, for the "instant transitions" that are no longer possible. Transitions today are more like car washes. We are tossed through them for a long period of time until we emerge on the other side, only to find that the job isn't finished and we have to rub that last little spot when we get home. Transitions are long, ambiguous, and messy. Yet they still occur, and they are, by and large, successful.

In young adulthood, we traverse many of the car washes of transition. Emergence from adolescence, moving out of the parental house, beginning the working life, changing jobs, changing cities, marriage, and parenthood all happen to people during young adulthood (although now it is more common for the last two to be delayed until one's mid-adult life). Without rituals to bury our old roles and baptize our new ones, we young adults are often adrift without vivid conceptions of our place in society. Our life states are ambiguous. We have moved out but are still financially dependent on our parents.

We have become parents ourselves but are scrambling to figure out what a parent ought to be. In the midst of all this, church and society often aren't exactly sure what to do with us.

Oftentimes good communication with older adults who have made such transitions can help us figure out our bearings. Sometimes, however, we find ourselves in a world so different from that of those who went before that we have to find our own way. Examples are young women beginning careers or people being the first in their family to receive a college education. In such cases, we have to be willing to explore and decide; to take life seriously, but not too seriously; to try, fail, and try again. This is difficult but exciting! We have opportunities our parents and grandparents never had. We have second and third chances that their more fixed society did not allow.

We must watch, though, that we do not try to do it all on our own. A support group of friends or associates is essential. Who among us wants to go through a tough transition alone? Despite our individualist ethos, we find it helpful to know that others are experiencing the same things. Some young adults want to know if others have found their first postcollege jobs unfulfilling. And aren't we smarter as a group than we are on our own? Discussion of transitions leads to better management of them. We can pool our experiences.

Let us not forget, either, that we need each other to keep us laughing. An "after-college group" I know gathered one Christmas and presented awards to those who had held the most number of jobs in the years since graduation and those who had worked at temp agencies the longest. The quest for employment can be difficult, but it revives us and lends perspective to keep laughing about it!

An inevitable advantage and disadvantage of contemporary life is mobility. Many of the transitions we undertake in our lives will require moving to a new place and leaving old support networks behind. Faced with an all new environment, it is important to seek new support systems—to build new friendships, meet different people—while we continue as well to depend on old friends and family via the telephone, letters, and visits. To go through transitions alone is a miserable prospect. We need to be able to talk about it.

Accentuate the Positive

One of the occupational hazards of examining the different burdens of young adulthood is negativity. Looking through the preceding pages, we might be tempted to throw in the spiritual towel. We've got transitions to face, self-discovery to attain, naiveté to dispel, and God-knows-how-many expectations to fulfill. Yet each of these has a positive side, a silver lining, as it were. The expectations of others sometimes help us to find the best way for ourselves. With naiveté also comes idealism, sincerity, and a positive attitude. Self-discovery is a fascinating journey, full of new life and new ways of understanding. Transitions afford us opportunities to start over, the chance to improve our lives and uncover new people and places. All of these things are burdens, no one will deny that. In a sense, however, they are also supplies and amenities. They make the spiritual journey better, more fun, an ever-expanding sightseeing tour of the road of faith.

Chapter Six: KEEPING OUR EYE ON THE BALL—DEALING WITH THE DISTRACTIONS OF YOUNG ADULTHOOD

I'm sure I was not the worst outfielder in the history of Little League, but maybe "I could have been a contender" if it had not been for the municipal airport next to the baseball fields. Out in right or center field, I would carefully observe the Cessnas take off and land. This would have been fine if I were meant to chart the Cessnas instead of catch the fly balls that came my way. Needless to say, the errors on my hypothetical baseball card multiplied.

I bring this up because in many ways faith is a matter of keeping your eye on the ball. Faith requires focus, as we saw earlier. There are all kinds of distractions in life, and many of these keep our focus away from the matter of spiritual growth. They keep us from finding our mature faith. Sometimes they are dramatic distractions—like drug and alcohol addiction, or membership in a cult or gang—but more often they are normal, healthy things that have gone too far—planning for the future, fantasy life, religion, worry, sex. In too generous doses, they absorb our attention, diverting us from the search for God's will in our lives. Our best energy is robbed, and we have little left to give to our own spiritual growth. In other words, distractions steal from us the first important supply on the spiritual journey—awareness. Nearly every spiritual tradition speaks of awareness as a foundation of the spiritual life. Without it, there often comes a day of reckoning. And there I am, "staring at the airplanes."

Sex

Lest we get off on the wrong foot, I want to begin by stating clearly that sex and sexuality are good. By sex I mean here the variety of sexual activity (from caresses to lovemaking) basic to human beings. By sexuality I mean that complex of sensations, feelings, desires, images, and thoughts that mark us as embodied beings and that draw us to one another. Both of these must be seen unequivocally as positive gifts of our loving God. Too much of our Western spirituality has been body-negative and antisexual, making us feel as if we ought to be embarrassed on account of our having bodies and being attracted to one another.

If spirituality is about the whole of our journey toward God and other people, then sexuality is a part of it. Sexual self-discovery is a key route along the road of faith. Our sexuality is like a delicate flower that longs to open and be known. We need touch. We long to share with others our deepest thoughts and feelings. Inner voices call us to explore and discover our sexual identity and preferences. We bypass these things only at great spiritual cost. Isolation, rage, self-hatred, and disconnection with self are only some of the fruits of disregarding them. On the other hand, the benefits of a successful struggle with ourselves as sexual beings are maturity, a good self-image, comfort with ourselves as physical beings, and healthy interaction with other physical beings.

There is, of course, a dark side to everything, including sex and sexuality. Sex can become a distraction in our lives, an energy-absorbing fixation that keeps us from dealing with the rest of our lives. We have all experienced one side of this or the other, I would bet. If we have not experienced the fixation of sexual obsessions, then we have suffered the unconscious fixation of sexual denial. When obsessed, we talk, think, and act out sex so much that it rules our lives (and perhaps puts us in danger as well). When immersed in denial, we expend an inordinate amount of energy trying to avoid dealing with some part of our sexuality. In the first case, the extreme is sexual addiction. The sexual addict cannot survive too long without sexual activity of some sort. On the other side, the extreme is frigidity or asexuality. Oftentimes, this is the product of childhood sexual trauma, a severely repressed family background, or repressed homosexuality. In either case, the afflicted person needs the help of a counselor, psychotherapist, special support group, or some combination thereof.

Because this is not a professional psychological work, our focus is not on these two ends of the sexual continuum. We are concerned here with the vast majority of us living somewhere between obsession and denial. Some of us find ourselves subtly buying into the old dualistic worldview, where the soul is good and holy, and the body is evil and ought to be ignored. Others of us find our way quietly to the conviction that sex is the key to happiness in life, that its attainment is the supreme goal (certainly many of us men were brought up to think this way). Sex is very important, but it is not the central purpose of life (Dr. Freud, call your office). One might say that it is "part of a balanced diet," but one could not realistically call it the essential nutrient.

Not that such a truth is easy to live. As young adults, we are biologically programmed to perpetuate the race. Our hormones are raging. We fall in love and lose all sense. And yet where sexuality is concerned, the call is for balance and integration. Not easy but not impossible either.

Our Endless Possibilities

As young adults today, we have more opportunities for different life choices than any other generation in the history of this planet. Unlike the multitudes of people that came before us, many of us today can choose our life situations from literally thousands of possibilities. We are told when we are young, "You can do anything you want in this life."

This is certainly an exciting blessing, but it can become a distraction as well. As exciting as a large field of possibilities may be, it is not so glamorous to make decisions and construct real-life situations out of possibilities. This is a long-term project; and it requires creativity, patience, discipline, hope, and fortitude. Not surprisingly, we can easily direct our attention and energy away from this longer term project and back to the consideration of possibilities. Instead of striking out on a career path, I can do odd jobs while indecisively turning over career possibilities in my head. Or I can move around frequently, unable to remain in one place for long. After all, there are so many wonderful places to live!

As entertaining as "playing the field" in this manner may be for a while, in the long run it distracts us from spiritual growth. We "spin our wheels" and don't get anything done. Instead, wise people recommend, our best bet is to choose an option that seems suitable for us and give it a shot. We may find this is not our way of living and have to start over, but that is all right. Better to learn by doing than to soar about the heavens, meditating on possibilities that will never come to life.

Shopping for Thrills

Everyone likes the feeling of a rush of adrenaline. Some of us like to roll down the windows of the car to feel the wind in our hair. Others like to watch a scary movie. I love roller coasters myself. We love a good thrill, and what is wrong with that? Nothing, unless it gets out of hand. There are young adults who like the adrenaline rush so much they live at constant emotional extremes. They begin to believe that a state of emotional intensity is to be desired all the time. Some attend heavy drinking parties several nights a week. Some take drugs, some take high-powered business jobs, some drive too fast.

Thrill-seeking becomes a distraction from life rather than a little play time when we begin to develop the expectation that all of life should be thrilling. This kind of thinking brings about devastating consequences. We refuse all relationships that are not "intense," that do not draw us into constant emotional extremes. We will not pray unless it brings a "spiritual high." Only intense, right-at-the-deadline work satisfies us. Regular meals, days, and habits make us feel bored and listless. The desire for a "rush" becomes a compulsion, necessary for our happiness.

Well, life is supposed to be exciting, isn't it? The truth, as most of us know deep down, is yes and no. Life does contain many "highs," surprises, and moments of great intensity; but too much intensity brings a heart attack, not wisdom or spiritual fulfillment. God calls us to a fulfilled, integrated, and balanced life. And we need to work at that. Some thrills will come with it and some more easygoing times as well. The key to the latter comes with the investment of our attention. Not all that is interesting and fulfilling comes in sound bites and rapid, exciting twists and turns. Some of the best things in life are moving at less than sixty miles per hour! It's about stopping and smelling the flowers, appreciating everything around us.

Addiction

We are now in the "age of recovery," according to some observers. Twelve-step groups have proliferated, so that now people can admit their powerlessness over a variety of addictions and compulsions. What began with Alcoholics Anonymous (AA) now includes Sex and Love Addicts Anonymous (SLAA), Narcotics Anonymous (NA), Cocaine Anonymous (CA), Overeaters Anonymous (OA), and a variety of other groups dealing with addictions such as compulsive shopping and gambling. Are all these groups one big scam? Ask the average participant, and you will find that the vast majority are not. Rather, they are a powerful testament to the control that addictions have over the human soul.

Addictions are, as one person put it, "the granddaddy of all spiritual distractions." They demand the bulk of our attention. Yet they are subtle, insidious. They do not always take the form of the stereotypical town drunk or spaced-out drug addict. More often, they are lying in the shadows. Usually not even the addict himself is aware. Yet the clues are there for those who have eyes to see. The middle-aged man who cannot get through the evening without a drink or two; the teenager who has been acting differently lately, whose grades have begun to drop; the young woman who sits down to dinner with a friend and pays more attention to the menu than to the friend—a perceptive observer can find the signs of addiction, for the compulsion, whatever it may be, will inevitably distract an addict from the rest of his life. The person will lose track of things—things perhaps not easily traced to the addiction—old levels of energy, personality traits, job performance, the ability to connect with other people in a meaningful way.

More to our point here, an addicted person will lose track of her faith. Addiction demands that the environment be controlled so that the addict can satisfy her craving. It leaves no place for the leap of faith, for a trust that God will be there. In fact, it takes the place of God, becoming a person's whole reason for living! Worse still, its power to distract from true spirituality extends beyond the addict herself to the entire family or community involved with the person. The focus of the family becomes protecting the addict's problem with a conspiracy of silence and denial rather than mutual care, support, and growth. It's a lose-lose scenario for spirituality! Indeed, if Jesus had lived in the "age of recovery," he might have said, "You cannot serve both God and your addiction."

I don't mean to provide a comprehensive guide to overcoming addiction here. There are plenty of good books on this (see the appendix). I would only add that addiction is a compulsion: the person cannot stop the drinking, the smoking, the gambling, on his own. Professional treatment or therapy is nearly always required. Absolutely required is the formulation of a program for recovery in conjunction with regular attendance of twelve-step meetings. The recovering addict must have the support of others who are struggling alongside him or her. It has become popular in some religious groups to attempt to conquer alcoholism and drug addiction without the support of treatment or twelve-step groups, simply by "turning it over to the Lord." This is deceiving. It seems to depend on God's love completely, as we all should; however, in reality, a kind of spiritual machismo is involved. "I don't need anyone's help but God's." This goes against our Christian tradition, for we have long believed that God's help comes to us primarily through the love of other people.

Codependence

In the age of recovery, *codependence* is another term thrown around as if it were a psychological mantra. Suddenly, everything is codependence. There is even a critique of contemporary therapy entitled *I'm Codependent, You're Codependent.* We have to be cautious with this word, yet it does draw our attention to a real issue. Some of us have been taught to become enmeshed with other people. We have been taught by our family of origin or by our culture to disregard emotional boundaries between ourselves and other people. When contemplating going to a movie, we do not ask, "What would I like to see?" Rather, we find out what others would like to see and assume that this is also our preference. We cannot tell the difference between what we want and what others want! Someone has told us that this is what love is. Yet love is a decision to intentionally give of myself to someone else. Of what do I give if I cannot tell where my self ends and someone else's begins?

Again, this is not the place to go into this in depth. There are several good books on the topic (see the appendix). I only broach the topic here to point out that codependence is a distraction along the road of faith. We become so fixated on the needs and feelings of others that we cannot focus on our own spiritual growth. And it keeps us from truly learning how to love.

Religious Distractions on the Road of Faith

How in the world can religion be a distraction to spirituality? Quite easily, as it turns out. In the introduction, we made the distinction between faith and religion. Faith is our trust in God. Christians believe that God gives faith; it is a gift to the individual believer and the community. We also believe that faith involves a response to God's gift—each of us has to seek to grow in that faith, to do the spiritual "work" that assists the development of our faith. Religion, on the other hand, is that system of practices and institutions that goes along with our response to God in faith. We need it. In the real concrete world, our faith life is going to require some organization, some rules and institutions. Intrinsically, however, religion is neither good nor bad; it depends on how it serves our faith life. Thus, some of the trappings of religion can be quite distracting to our journey toward God. They are exactly the type of religion we need to lose!

Superstition

We are all superstitious to some extent. None of us feels good when a mirror breaks, and nearly everyone can get "spooked" by tales of supernatural events. Yet superstition can get out of hand, and then it becomes a distraction to real faith. Consider one of the most frequent culprits of superstitious distraction that absorbs some people's attention excessively—the devil. People ingest by the thousands stories of possession, child-killing cults, repressed ritual abuse memories, and various activities of Satan and his cohorts amongst us. This sort of obsession travels under the nomenclature of "spiritual warfare" in some circles. Demonic overlords are poised to take over our cities and towns, they believe, and we must pray like warriors to fend them off.

Now, surely prayer is a valuable resource in the human struggle against evil. Who would debate or deny this? But this focus on the demonic is misplaced. All that energy could be used for spiritual growth, community-building, thinking about God. Moreover, the predominance of this sort of thinking about evil distracts us from real, dangerous, comprehensive evils—widespread poverty, social injustice, racism, war, the devaluation of human life, ecological disasters, and so forth. It blinds us to the unjust structures of society, the marginalization of people about which Jesus spoke so much during his lifetime.

The "devil" distraction tends to be a superstition of evangelical Protestants, but lest those of us from the Catholic tradition think we are immune from such distractions, consider this. Equally distracting to mature faith are some Roman Catholic superstitions concerning certain recent appearances of Mary around the world. To call attention to this is not to devalue the importance of the Blessed Mother in Roman Catholic tradition or to argue against legitimate honor given to Mary. Nor is it even to make a judgment against all Marian apparitions. The problem is that many Catholics are so involved with the "revelations" and "appearances" of Mary that their spirituality ends there. They are so fascinated by alleged supernatural occurrences surrounding these appearances that they assume that this ought to be the focus of our faith in these times.

Fortunately, we have the voices of saints and mystics over the centuries affirming that visions and supernatural events are no more important than the *daily* revelations of God's presence in our ordinary lives. They are certainly much less important than the key revelation of our faith, Jesus. These voices of wisdom from our tradition, such as that of St. Teresa of Avila, remind us to be on guard lest allegedly (or truly, for that matter) supernatural events distract us from the business at hand, growing together in our trust of God.

And then there is the "Trifold Test." Catholic tradition always cautions us not to put our trust in any religious experience unless it passes three tests. It must pass the test of time; that is, its effects and memory must linger. Then, there is the test of reality, the stipulation that the religious experience must be able to survive in the real world; it should not require creating an illusion world for its adherents. Third and most important, any such event must pass the test of charity. It must lead people to become more loving, more inclusive, more charitable toward all of their fellow human beings.

Fundamentalism as Distraction

Fundamentalism is the Empire State Building of religious distractions for young adults. Particularly on college campuses and among down-and-out young people, it preys on our trust and inexperience in matters of religion. Its partisans present an attractive package—a tight-knit group of passionate believers with rock-solid, black-and-white certainty about matters of faith and religion. Using an emotional experience of submission to Jesus as Lord as sure sign of salvation, they take a narrow and limited view of the Scriptures, concentrating on biblical stories as literal facts and isolated quotes taken out of context. They often overlook the overall themes and figurative messages, the "big picture," in favor of these smaller segments. Thus, on the surface, they seem to be taking a healthy interest in the Bible. Unfortunately, their superficial literalism leads people into a relationship with "the Book" rather than with Christ. Many Catholics especially, infamous for our poor knowledge of Scripture, get taken in. Furthermore, we buy into their structured, easy answers to the big questions of life—identifying faith with an emotional experience, placing science and culture in opposition to religion, believing hell to be the destiny of all who choose another path. Perhaps it is a longing for security in a chaotic world that attracts us. Maybe we are afraid of perishing in hell. Whatever draws us in, once captured by these notions, we easily forget the complexities of life, of the scriptures. We lose sight of the spiritual journey with its uncertainty and of the need for trust in God; and we opt instead for the "spiritual elevator" that zooms us up to the lair of an arbitrary but clearly seen God.

Despite its appeal, biblical fundamentalists do have vocal detractors in our society, and many young Christians have become wise to their tactics and stay away from their street-corner evangelists, college campus groups, and small exclusive churches. There is, however, a less-known brand of fundamentalism in my own Roman Catholic Church as well. Though it does as much harm as the Protestant equivalent, it does not always breed the same opposition. In the absence of such opposition, young Catholics can be taken in. Just as with biblical fundamentalism, it provides security, certainty, and easy answers to difficult questions. In the place of a naive faith in the scriptures, however, it demands uncritical acceptance of whatever comes from the mouth of traditional authorities— priests, nuns, bishops, the pope. Mature Catholics, of course, pay attention to such authorities, but they also think carefully and critically about what they say. Catholic fundamentalists pine for pre-Vatican II days when (they think) everything was clear and no variety or dissent was tolerated. Often their spirituality depends on arbitrary rules and practices rather than on a faithful embrace of the risky roads of the spiritual journey. Sniffing them out consists mainly in applying the second of the Trifold Tests: Does their religious faith pass the test of reality? Does it contradict what we see and know to be true about our world, or does it create a world of its own?

Cults

A short word about cults is unfortunately necessary. While fundamentalist groups are distractions along the road of faith, cults are dead ends. We need only think back a few years to the David Koresh episode in Waco, Texas for this point to become evident. Each year, cults claim a large number of young people, stealing them away from their families and friends. They demand complete and uncritical obedience to leaders with delusions of grandeur. They teach people to suppress their individual identities to merge into the robot army of the cult. The result is a complete halt of the spiritual journey, a turning off onto a road that leads to dangerous spiritual places.

The lure of a cult is its sense of belonging. We all desire to belong, to be part of a close-knit group of human beings. Thus, most cults prey on people when they are lonely and under severe psychological stress—after a death in the family, an arrival in a new place, the end of a relationship, a job loss. The welcoming atmosphere the group provides feels like salvation, a chance to start over and be accepted. The recruiting members hide the cost in the beginning, but gradually the incoming member learns that her individuality must be submerged so that she may submit more fully to group expectations. Meanwhile, the new recruit is systematically cut off from outside relationships—including parents and friends—until she is totally dependent on the cult for emotional and physical support.

Cults do not pass any of the Trifold Tests. They have no sense of tradition or of being tested by time. They cannot coexist with the rest of reality and so must cut off their members from their old worlds. Most importantly, they do not lead people to a more charitable existence. They serve the self-interests of a charismatic founder or some kind of "junta" of leaders. Cults are about power and prestige for the leadership and childlike subservience and psychological destruction for the adherents.

Conclusion: Negativity

Surprisingly, the spiritual distraction voted "most likely to succeed" is not cults or addiction or even sex. It is negativity. All too easily do we shift from "drive" on the road of faith to "reverse" in the endless downward spiral of negativity. All too easily do we give in to the human impulse to dwell on the negative, to whine and complain without ceasing.

The Five-Minute Rule: Everyone is permitted to complain for five minutes unimpeded. After that, he or she has to do some-thing about it.

For most of us, bucking the Five-Minute Rule is more of an occasional temptation than a chronic problem. It's about those moments when we decide to inflict our bad mood on everyone else. Or we sabotage a meeting conducted by someone with whom we are angry. Even when anger and fear are not at the top of our emotional list, negativity can still be a temptation and a distraction. Psychologist Mihaly Csikszentmihalyi notes that human beings have a built-in propensity for letting our consciousness collapse into what he calls "psychic entropy."[1] In other words, when we are psychically idle, our minds turn toward the negative. Why is this? It could be a matter of childhood wounds. Perhaps it is a product of living in a world with serious limits. Who knows? The important thing is to keep our spiritual antennae attuned to God's gifts in our lives, to the graces we do receive rather than the way our expectations are not met.

For some of us, negativity appears to be a more serious difficulty, a problem of disease-like proportions. These are the folks among us who can bring a dinner conversation to anger and fear within minutes. They can drag an entire group of people down with them into the pit of cynicism. An old priest I once knew was a member of this club. When greeted with "Good morning," he inevitably responded grimly, "I have other plans." With some delightful exceptions, his conversations centered around the many years of hurt and error he had seen go by in his religious community.

How does a person get this bad? A possible explanation goes something like this. Life involves pain and suffering. There are no alternative options on that. Part of the spiritual journey involves working through this pain. That means finding ways to constructively express the strong emotions that go along with hurt—anger, disappointment, sadness, severe frustration. Some of us journal, some share with family and friends, and some take our hurt feelings to prayer before our God. Others of us channel the emotions into athletics and art. For the more difficult moments, many seek the help of a trained psychotherapist.

Whatever it is that we do, we have to do it. Otherwise, the emotions get stuffed. Inside us they stagnate. Our health may suffer; headaches and gastrointestinal problems often result from stuffed emotions. But perhaps the more dangerous outcome of stuffed emotions is descending into a more-or-less permanent state of negativity. Filled with hurt and bitterness, we declare ourselves victims in a hostile world. We complain. We have trouble finding the positive side of situations. Most troubling, we bring other people down with us. Negative, cynical remarks can sabotage almost any meeting or project. This severe type of negativity is a progressive disease. Unless we do something to curb it, it takes over our perspective. We begin to see everything in pejorative terms. Our whole reality becomes circumscribed by our collapse into victimhood. We cannot move to change ourselves or anything else. There is no growth, no progress on the road to mature faith. It is a deadly distraction.

For a person deeply immersed in this distraction, much spiritual work is necessary. A little psychological Drano is needed for the emotional clog. The person has to learn to open up and begin to trust again. Moreover, he needs a big dose of the antidote to this poison—perspective. Perspective enables us to see that suffering is part and parcel of the human condition. None of us deserve it and it is frequently unjust, but we all have to deal with it. Life is not just suffering, however. Life is joy and peace and fun! Life contains moments of profound learning, deep intimacy, wild celebration. As Christians, we believe that all of life, every good thing that we have, is a gift from God. It is only when we lose track of that fundamental insight that we begin to look at the world as an enemy that victimizes its inhabitants.

Chapter Seven: TRANSFORMING OUR EXPECTATIONS

There is a well-known Buddhist saying, "If you meet the Buddha on the road, kill him." The Western corollary might be, "If you have God or even life all figured out, then you don't yet know anything." The underlying idea here is that every human being comes equipped with false expectations about reality and that these expectations die slowly and grudgingly. Each of us believes that she or he has a handle on everything; if we did not, we probably would go crazy with fear and anxiety. Yet, as St. Paul says, "Now we see indistinctly, as in a mirror" (1 Cor 13:12). Our view of reality is not yet complete. We are going to be surprised, continually, throughout our lives. Our expectations about God, about ourselves, about all of reality will have to change, to be transformed. The good news is, that's what Christianity is all about. We call it conversion. God takes everything we thought we knew about reality and turns it upside down. In this way, God teaches us surrender, the humble openness to the Holy Spirit that is mature faith.

The expectations about life that young adults are called upon to give up in the course of our lives are legion. They make up the "old religion" that we have to let go of if we seek a truer faith. From the myriad of expectations, this chapter comments on three that are reported by many young adults—perfectionism, the "convenient" life, and material prosperity over emotional prosperity. These expectations, for most people, will not stand up when reality strikes. Hardship, failure, and career and family responsibilities come to everyone. Many saints and mystics say that God actually uses these to pull the proverbial rug from beneath us. Only then can we take a fresh look at the world around us and see for the first time what God has in store for us. Yes, there are difficulties and sufferings, but there is also much faith, hope, and love. And this is not to mention the awesome possibilities of a world transformed by God, a world we would call the reign of God.

From Perfectionism to Integration

An academic counselor recently told me an interesting story about one of her students. After a string of semesters where he earned decent but not stellar grades, this young man embarked on an all-out crusade to earn a perfect grade point average. He reduced his work hours, virtually eliminated his social life, cut back on sleep and exercise, and abandoned all his extracurricular commitments. After an intense and anguished semester, he received his grades in the mail only to find that he had not done appreciably better. The grades were more or less the same. Unable to achieve academic perfection, the student nearly had a breakdown. He did not know what else to do. He had not counted failure into the equation! Unfortunately, his academic counselor informed me, this type of thing is all too common. She told me how hard it is to convince certain students that measured expectations, a balanced life, and taking care of oneself make for a better life.

Perfectionism is clearly the problem here. Somewhere along the path of life, many of us have learned that failure makes a person a second-class citizen. No less than perfection is required. I must succeed completely in all I do. If something is difficult—studies, social life, work, a relationship—I put all my energy into it and neglect the rest of my life. The end results are predictable. No matter what I do, I will feel a restless dissatisfaction (I haven't done everything I could have). In the long run, I will experience stress and frustration because I expect and strive for what I can never have—total success. The fundamental problem here has to do with my value as a person; we perfectionists build our self-esteem on our ability to succeed. We do the tasks with which we are charged, and we have learned to expect that their successful completion will validate us as human beings. Thus when we fail (and we will fail), our sense of self-worth is destroyed. Our whole life is doing, and failure means we did not do well.

But in reality, all of life is not doing. Ultimately, *being* is more important than doing. Who we are is more important than what we do. In other words, our worth as human beings is innate—it was and is a free gift of God (Gn 1:26–31). Once we internalize this idea, we can begin to recognize and deal with our limitations. As human beings, each of us will have many limits—of physical strength, intelligence, and beauty; of dexterity, skills, ability to learn, and so forth. The perfectionist looks at all these and says, "Why couldn't God give me more?" The person who knows her worth in God's eyes looks at these and says, "Praise God!"

When we are rooted in who we are, in who God has made us, we appreciate what we can do and actually celebrate our limitations. In addition, we accept that we have made mistakes and brought sin into our lives by our own bad choices. Aware of this, we commit ourselves to doing better. These are the benefits to accepting our worth in God's eyes. But they certainly do not come easy; they require a lifetime of work and transformation by God. Day by day, when we really look at the way our lives work, we realize something important: We need not strive for perfection. Instead, we strive for integration, accepting the bad and the good in us and striving to give the good the upper hand.

From a Life of Ease to a Life of Growth

We live in the most affluent culture in the world, and we have the "stuff" to prove it—microwave ovens, remote control television, electric kitchen utensils, home exercise equipment, computers, cellular phones, automobiles. To keep the "stuff" selling and moving, advertisers must persuade us that we need their wares, that our lives would be incomplete without them. They elevate convenience to requirement. Growing up in a media culture, as most of us today have, we absorb this rhetoric and begin to buy into a deadly expectation—that life is supposed to be convenient and comfortable. If you are really living well, life is easy.

Now life usually destroys that expectation with little fanfare. Life is not convenient or easy. Traffic jams happen. People are sometimes rude. Machines break down. People break down. Crying children and the weather do not check to see if their timing is right before they demand our attention. More tragically, death and illness occur. Intimate relationships fail. People leave each other, and the loss is devastating. It is these events that finish off our "life is easy" expectation. In the case of the more tragic events, we hurt more than we ever thought we could hurt, and it is never at a convenient time.

How do people deal with the demise of the "easy life"? Some try to deny it entirely, but this does not last long. Others escape into the various distractions described in the previous chapter. A peculiarly American strategy is to accumulate "stuff" to insulate us from the world and its problems. This strategy actually goes a long way. Those of us in middle to upper socioeconomic levels can live in suburban enclaves away from most criminal activity, poverty, and neighborhood violence. We have cars, computers, and other conveniences to allow us to do what we need with minimal problems. In our society, money can buy a certain degree of control over life. But it cannot protect us from all hardships. It breaks down in the face of emotional, physical, and interpersonal problems. It cannot save us from loneliness or disaster. Its ability to stave off the pain of life is decidedly limited.

Recognizing that much of life's pain and inconvenience can be traced back to our dealings with other people, some of us look to insulate ourselves emotionally from other human beings. We "put on a happy face" or hide in the corners of public gatherings, hoping that our fragile masks will protect us from the difficulties of human relationships. This too goes a long way. Being alone minimizes the pain of relationships and increases the amount of control I have over my life. But few find it worth the consequences. Human beings were meant to live in relationship and community. Isolation kills us inside. Loneliness and alienation eventually drive us to seek company or to turn to some kind of "fix" to compensate.

With what choice are we left then? We have to learn to roll with the punches and see things as they are, not as we would like them to be. Our best bet is to change our expectation of ease to a more realistic expectation—that life is a challenge and a constant opportunity to grow. The wisest among us, both older and younger, already know this. People realize that life is a struggle, an arduous but worthwhile process. We can expect hardship and tragedy as well as joy and success. The question we ask along the road of faith is "What can I learn from this? Where is God leading me? Is there something here with which I must come to terms? Is there some injustice here that I must resist?" Our experience of life's struggle, of the ups and downs, provides us with raw material for reflection and prayer. God is always calling on us to grow, to convert. The question emerges from our lives: "Where is God leading me today?"

From Material Goods to Emotional Goods

Perhaps one of the most ironic situations of our modern American society is a certain reversal of expectations. In the days when people lived in smaller communities and family members worked at home, people had certain expectations that their extended families and neighbors would provide for their emotional needs. A sense of belonging and self-worth, a feeling of emotional security—these "emotional goods" came primarily from the family, and a person requested them of his or her family. At the same time, people of that time did not have great expectations in terms of material wealth. For most people, having their basic needs met was enough. Today we have it reversed. We expect a high number of material goods but not many emotional ones.

It is unlikely that we can go back to a situation where our biological family members provide for all our emotional needs. Our nuclear families are too small for this, and most extended families are scattered. Still, we need primary relationships where these needs can be satisfied. We need to learn to ask people to make us feel welcome, to hold us, to care for us when we are ill or psychologically fatigued. We have to develop quality friendships where we can ask for these things. This is particularly difficult for men. We spend much of our time with superficial friends who often drag us down with competition, negativism, and insecurity. Oftentimes we need a kick in the behind to go out there and cultivate friendships with people who nurture and challenge us instead of just putting us down. For me, it took an insightful boot from a good spiritual director, someone who only knew my friends from what I told her about them! When I did change my ways and seek true friendships, I found some that endure through time and over distance. Such friendships are more than worth the effort they require!

Where do we go to find such friends? They can be found anywhere, but a good strategy is to get involved with a community of faith. There are no guarantees, but a strong, vibrant faith community (not a dull, dead one) will usually involve other young adults who want to grow in faith, hope, and love.

Chapter Eight: SPIRITUAL SUPPLIES

Once we've made a conscious commitment to living a life of faith, what do we need on our end to make it work? What kind of habits will help us to be open to God's call in our lives? What are the spiritual supplies necessary for a mature faith? From my own experience and that of friends and various folks I know, I offer the following list. You might say they are some (though not all) of the "habits of spiritually effective people."

Another way to think about it is by returning to the journey paradigm. The key to good traveling is not traveling light or traveling heavy but taking along exactly what you need—no more, no less. We spoke earlier about some of the burdens young adults carry along the road of faith and how we get weighed down with these unnecessary accessories. There are also supplies we've *got* to have for best results along the way. This chapter is about those essential supplies.

Awareness

In almost all spiritual traditions, the first movement is to awareness. The Indian Jesuit Anthony de Mello often remarked that awareness was the first step in learning how to pray. At a retreat I attended, one college student put it like this:

> You know, we go through most of our lives asleep. I don't even notice half the time how wonderful my friends and family are. And being out here in nature has reminded me that God is truly everywhere, but I forget, I space out. This retreat has been like a wake-up call for me.

God is all around us, but many of us are too preoccupied to notice. Take it from a recovering "space cadet." But we all suffer from the disease from time to time. We get caught up in our work, our worries, our lofty thoughts and ambitions. We think about yesterday, long ago, tomorrow, and the distant future, but we do not remember to live today.

Test yourself at random moments. Do you know what is going on in your environment? Is it spring and are plants flowering? Is the sky a peculiar shade of blue today? Is that family sitting next to you on the bus shabbily dressed? What is your friend's body language telling you as you converse? Awareness begins with the physical events that surround us. From there we move to awareness of what things mean— tones and body language, unusual appearances, new events. We also become aware of how God is involved in all this. God the Holy Spirit is constantly at work in the world— renewing it, communicating to us through it, endowing it with beauty and life. But we cannot begin to know God in our environment unless we first notice our environment.

Discipline

Discipline strikes many people as an ugly word. It conjures up images of unpleasant duties and painful persistence. It reminds people of things they *have to do* that take them away from the things they *want to do*.

Yet discipline is the motor oil of the spiritual journey—without a steady supply, the different parts of our lives will not run at all. We know that there are many things within us and without us that dull our progress toward a mature faith. Discipline keeps our positive movements going even when these obstacles intervene. In particular, discipline protects us from the effects of depression, apathy, and laziness. We are all prone to wanting to give up, to throw in the towel, to sit back and wait rather than engaging life and living to the fullest. Discipline means cultivating the good habits and healthy patterns of living that keep us going even when the going gets tough. Discipline ensures that we have good eating habits and regular exercise. It calls for a healthy daily engagement in our work or study. It bids us maintain regular quality contact with our closest friends or family members. And to really make the most of our spiritual journey, it asks for a daily personal prayer life as well as participation in communal prayer. In essence, discipline helps us to keep practicing our faith. This is usually associated with the last of the aforementioned habits, but ironically, all of these disciplines are practicing our faith, since faith is the glue that holds all parts of our lives together. Holiness, the goal of faith, is essentially wholeness, getting my whole life together and placing it before God.

Since a holistic sense of discipline is clearly an asset, how do we keep at bay a negative view of discipline? How do we keep from seeing our good habits and patterns as dull duties that we must perform to get our passing grade in Spirituality 101? Creativity helps. We can vary the ways in which we exercise and pray. And we can conduct frequent "attitude checks." Do we see cooking balanced meals as a chore or a culinary adventure? Is making contact with a close friend who's far away a hassle or a terrific opportunity? One way or another, we have to keep discipline in a positive light, for discipline is the key to all the other spiritual supplies. With discipline, we learn to build and keep good habits.

Enjoyment of the Ordinary

Much of spirituality is learning to appreciate the simple beauties and pleasures God has given us in each moment. This is not a Hallmark card!   I'm serious. Some say that grandiose special effects and fast-paced action have snuffed out young adults' ability to notice the ordinary, but I can't believe that. Still, it could not hurt us to strengthen the habit, lest the "sound-bite mentality" edit out some of the more precious yet inconspicuous gifts of God.

It all begins, as was said earlier, with awareness, with attention to the ordinary things of life—to plants, wallpaper, eye color, cloud shapes, the little eccentricities of our loved ones. Taking note of such things can reveal them to us in new ways. If we are willing to be patient enough, we can learn things about the ordinary that we never knew. The last few days I have been noticing that a household plant keeps turning toward the sun coming through the window, no matter how many times it gets bumped and moved.

Even if we don't gain actual insights, learning to enjoy the ordinary is an activity of immense spiritual profit. For God, as the saying goes, is in the details. If we search the Gospels, we discover that many of the stories told of Jesus are not extraordinary. They are not miracle healings or the horrifying drama of being betrayed by a friend. They are short conversations Jesus had with Nicodemus (Jn 3:1–21) or Zacchaeus (Jn 19: 1–10). They are folk stories Jesus told with a slight twist (parables). They are dinner conversations, visits with friends, instructions to his disciples. These were all ordinary moments. They became extraordinary because the Evangelists saw them as times when God was at work in the world in Jesus.

God is at work in the ordinary parts of our lives too. Consider fidelity. Whether it be to a friend, lover, or family member, fidelity is played out in ordinary nondramatic time, in the daily and weekly ministries of mutual presence. Yet so many people (and the church in the ritual celebration of marriage) find it a significant expression of God's love in their lives. God is in the details! We can see the same thing in the way a believing scientist looks at minutiae in her field or the way simple words carry away readers of poetry. Learning to appreciate the ordinary is a way to find God.

Courage and Initiative

I read a story in the newspaper about a runner who drove across town to participate in a 10K run. Unfortunately, she misread her directions and ended up at a marathon instead, though she did not realize this until the race had actually begun. About to drop out, she saw the Nike slogan on the back of the T-shirt on the man in front of her, "Just Do It." So she did. She kept running, and twenty-six miles later she finished the marathon.

The message of the story rings true for the spiritual journey as well. The most human of temptations is to avoid risk and stay in our "safety zones." It is important to have a modicum of security and stability in our lives. But life is always risky, especially the spiritual life. Developing the virtues of courage and initiative are key to maintaining a mature faith. Courage gives us the intestinal fortitude to face up to what we fear in search of a greater good. It is what enables the soldier to face death for the good of his country and the nonviolent resister to face imprisonment and harassment for that same country. It enables the young, family-centered student, terrified of leaving home, to depart for college in pursuit of education.

Courage calls us forward when fear calls us back. It is based on faith—trust that no matter how frightening life gets, God has brought us this far and will continue to guide us home. Initiative, on the other hand, is what gets us over the initial hump. Initiative pushes us into creative action when we would like to stall in our comfortable places. Like courage, it is a virtue or habit that grows through practice. Initiative allows the new employee to seek how to do her job better. It bids the dissatisfied student to search out a new major, perhaps something totally untried.

Initiative and courage take us places on the proverbial road of faith. By practicing these virtues, we are able to reach out to people in relationship. We turn our backs on unfulfilling careers and stop spending our leisure in unsatisfying ways. We refuse the lure of passive entertainment and opt instead for active and spontaneous fun. Keeping these virtues in practice in our lives isn't easy, but God calls us to it. God does not call us to take dangerous risks for stupid reasons or in hopeless situations. But the Lord of life wants us to get involved in life! God wants us to take chances, to make new friends, to ask questions and ponder problems, to break artificial barriers, to stand up and speak out against injustice. In this manner, we become dynamic forces in the world, making a better life for ourselves and for the common good.

Touch

Psychologists tell us that no human being can live without touch. Without that physical sensation of someone reaching out to me, I die—if not literally, then certainly emotionally. We know the power of touch. Imagine when, at the moment of deepest sorrow, a friend places her hand gently but firmly on your shoulder. With that simple gesture, you know that your friend has consented to journey with you through that difficult time. Touch can convey where language fails.

Most of the Christian sacraments make use of one form of touch or another to communicate what is deeply human and an occasion for God's grace to work among us. At confirmation, hands are laid upon the believer's head and then oil is smeared on his face. They are signs of the descent of the Holy Spirit, of empowerment for witness, of being chosen (as kings were anointed in ancient times). Could words convey so much?

Touch can encourage, support, heal, celebrate, express love, and give pleasure. On the other hand, it can also harm and destroy. Its power can be misused. The trust that we all desire from those we respect and love is betrayed when touch is used abusively or inappropriately. Even putting these more serious cases of abuse and assault aside, we must be careful with touch. People have different levels of comfort and safety with touch. What is invasive to me may be normal and appreciated from your point of view. Different regions and cultures have different ideas about touch as well. But with sensitivity, tolerance, and patience, touch will remain for us an important element of our faith journey.

A Sense of Humor

Sister José Hobday tells the story of how a particular line of Psalm 50 was translated in the old Douay-Rheims Catholic Bible. Verse 9 read, "I will accept no bull from your house." The reference is to God's unhappiness with Israel's animal sacrifices; Sister José, however, found the line equally true in the light of another meaning of "bull."

Life can be funny if we are open to seeing it that way.

Humor begins with irony, the strange contrast between what happens in life and what we expect. There is no shortage of this contrast along the road of faith! From co-workers' misconceptions to accidental puns to our own silly mistakes, there will be much to laugh at for those who want to.

There are even many brands of humor—the absurd, the sarcastic, and the silly; plays on words, visual comedy, comical stories, and so forth. Even religion can be funny, as Sister José reminds us. I recall a time when a friend was reciting a prayer that said, "Like incense from a brazier, Lord, let our prayer rise up to you." He got tongue-tied, however, and said, "Like incense from a brassiere, Lord..." After rolling on the floor for a few minutes, we were finally able to continue the prayer service.

Not only *can* faith be funny, it *ought* to be funny. We mentioned that humor is based on irony. No one is more ironic than God. This is the God who promises Abraham he will be the father of many nations, then proceeds to allow him two children, one who is banished. This God made the aged Elizabeth the mother of John the Baptist, told Ezekiel to hide his underwear near a river, made the number one persecutor of Christianity its most famous missionary (St. Paul), and chose a handyman from a backwater town in Galilee to be the savior of the world. God is surely ironic, and maybe seeing the humor in life can help us to better understand our strange God. Maybe humor is a kind of "school in faith." It lends enjoyment to faith, but it also lends perspective. It teaches us to appreciate the unpredictability and absurdity of life. When we learn to laugh at ourselves, humor schools us in letting go of our pretensions and accepting our limitations.

Finally, humor is a necessary way of expressing the depth and variety of human emotion. There are two things we know about funerals and funeral receptions—some will cry and some will laugh, both remembering the deceased. For all these reasons, we do well to cultivate humor in our lives. Even and especially in our faith lives. Laughter and joking around can be an important part of our prayer lives!

Passion and Enthusiasm

An evangelical friend of mine decided to give the Catholic Church a try. But she was afraid, she told me, that she would not find enough believers there who were "on fire for Christ." Although as a Catholic I was a bit offended by her incendiary language (pun intended), I had an inkling as to what she meant. She wanted to associate with other Christians who were passionate and enthusiastic believers. So I tried to assure her that although Catholics hardly ever use language like that, they do often have a passionate attachment to their faith.

Both enthusiasm and passion are important to mature faith. Enthusiasm is that energy of personality, that outward-directed, positive energy that we bring to life's endeavors. Stereotypically, it is the province of the young, but we have all met very enthusiastic older people as well. Enthusiasm is "energy for" something; people are enthusiastic workers, enthusiastic hobbyists, enthusiastic believers, enthusiastic organizers. We might think of enthusiasm as a short-term virtue; it cheers people up, jump-starts parties, gets people excited about projects, moves people to get involved in their religion. But it does not truly sustain people for the long haul. Passion, on the other hand, is the long-term virtue. Passion keeps us going through the ups and downs of life. While enthusiasm bids us commit our emotions to some end, passion requires our whole selves—body, mind, and spirit. Popular romance novels talk about "passion," usually meaning sexual desire; but real passion for someone is that commitment to a loved one that sustains the relationship in bad times and in good.

People sometimes ask young adults, "What's your passion?" In other words, what is it in your life that gives you energy, that you would rather do than anything else? The scholar of myths and legends Joseph Campbell speaks of how various myths teach people "to follow their bliss," to take up the cause or vocation or love that their whole being longs for. The poet Rainer Maria Rilke, in a letter to an aspiring writer, puts it like this:

> Go into yourself. Search for the reason that bids you write; find out whether it is spreading out its roots in the deepest places in your heart, acknowledge to yourself whether you would have to die if it were denied you to write. This above all—ask yourself in the stillest hour of your night: must I write?...if you may meet this earnest question with a strong and simple "I must," then build your life according to this necessity.[1]

However we articulate it, each of us needs a passion in our lives. We need to be committed to a greater good beyond ourselves, something we feel in our very bones. Different people have different passions. For some, it will be a cause, like obtaining better living conditions for poor people. Others will find passion in raising children. Still others will take on a vocation, a career and lifestyle that defines a part of who they are. Most of us will actually have several passions, and smaller passions that may or may not develop into larger concerns. Much of what young adulthood is about is uncovering what it is that we are passionate about. What talents has God placed in us for the common good? Among these, what gives us the most energy? These are the question we ask. Moreover, we seek advice from those who have found their passions, just as the young poet wrote to Rilke. We need the wisdom of those who have gone before us. Still, in the final analysis, it is we who must decide.

Whatever our other passions in life, our faith in God will be the most important in the long run. For when all else passes away, God, in whom we "live and move and have our being," as the Roman Catholic liturgy tells us, remains. No other passion in our lives will completely fill the longings of our hearts. They will partially satisfy us and will keep us full of life in younger years; but the wisdom and loneliness of our life in the long term will eventually call each of us, whatever our lifestyle and situation, to fall in love with God.

‖≡‖

Chapter Nine: COMPANIONS IN FAITH

A lot of people don't like to travel alone.

For most of us, the enjoyment of new places, people, and scenes is enhanced and enriched by the presence of companions. And so it is on the journey of faith, especially for young adults. Faith is such a "hush-hush" topic for us that we rejoice when we find out that friends, co-workers, professors, and potential "significant others" are actually believers! Attending services, we find ourselves reassured knowing that those around us are caught up in the same prayer to God. And who among us has not had that wonderful experience of sharing faith for the first time in the context of a growing friendship?

Though it is a wonderful blessing, companionship on the road of faith is not just spiritual frosting, a nice extra along the way. In reality, we need spiritual companionship. Individual faith by itself is largely a myth. We receive our faith from God through parents, teachers, friends, and mentors. It grows under the care and encouragement of others. We exercise the justice to which it calls us most effectively as a group. What faith could there be without communities of faith? Who would hand on the traditions, the lessons and experience of those who went before? Who would guide the children, support the old, encourage the young and energetic? Furthermore, the scriptures tell us, "Those who say, 'I love God,' and hate their brothers and sisters, are liars; for those who do not love brother or sister whom they have seen, cannot love God whom they have not seen" (1 Jn 4:20). The love of God and of neighbor is one; thus, we seek to love God in relationship with other people. For most of us, this comes down to making the spiritual journey in the context of a community of faith.

The Original Communities and Scripture

We know that faith does not come to each person magically, *deus ex machina,* from the sky. It is passed to us by those who came before us, and someone passed it on to them. The chain goes back to the original community of disciples. They were the ones who walked with the Lord, who saw his face, heard his words, despaired at his horrible death, and were transformed by his rising and by the coming of the Holy Spirit.

> What we have seen and heard
> we proclaim now to you,
> so that you too may have fellowship with us;
> for our fellowship is with the Father
> and with his Son, Jesus Christ.
>
> (1 Jn 1:3)

As far as we can tell, these original disciples were all Jewish. Thus, they brought all the traditions and writings of the Hebrew community to their newfound faith in Jesus. As they reflected more and more on the meaning of the life, death, and resurrection of their teacher, under the guidance and inspiration of the Holy Spirit, they shared the story of Jesus. As they traveled, they shared it beyond the Jewish community, and many Gentiles came to believe in Jesus as God's unique revelation to humankind.

As the years went on, the stories about Jesus and about these earliest disciples began to be told at Christian gatherings. They were remembered and passed around. Eventually, as the last eyewitnesses of Jesus' life, death, and resurrection died off, Christian communities decided that the story and the proclamation had to be preserved for future generations. So they gathered the stories that had been told and wrote them down. In this way, the Gospels were produced. They also edited and compiled some of the letters of famous missionaries, one from that first generation (Paul of Tarsus) and several from succeeding generations. Finally, stories from the earliest churches were added. As these stories and letters were collected and edited, they were adapted to address the questions and struggles of new generations of Christians, and they were passed around the different communities. Gradually, the church collected all of them together as the New Testament we have today. These new scriptures were added to the traditional Jewish scriptures, which had been honored and used by Christians all along.

Such was the birth of our scriptures. We recognize in them the written legacy of the Jewish community up to the time of Christ as well as the recorded heritage of first-century Christians. Passed down through the years to us, they are honored as inspired reflections on God's presence in the world. They remain a precious testimony to us today, forming and informing our Christian faith. Every faith journey is enhanced by their riches.

The scriptures are to be approached with care, to be sure; and we have to consider their historical context (and thus, their sometimes sexist and militaristic overtones). Commentaries and companion books help us wade through such

things.[1] Yet Christians also need to read the Bible itself, especially as a community. We need to reflect on its lessons, speak
together in our hearts its poetry in praise of God. It is the
beginning of our community's journey guided by the Holy
Spirit. Many of its words remain timeless, securing for us the
lessons of those first Christian churches.

Many Christians today read the scriptures as a part of their
prayer lives. One of the most common ways of doing this in
the Roman Catholic tradition is known as *lectio divina*. Lectio
divina is not Bible *study*. You do not read over a passage and
then try to understand what it means. Rather, you read the
passage slowly. You try to let the poetry of the words speak
to you, to feel what words are "heavier" than others. What
sticks out? What gives you pause? What feels like it is something you need to hear right now? It may be no more than a
simple phrase. Perhaps the phrase "Do not be afraid," found
in several stories of the Bible (e.g., Gn 15:1; Is 43:1; Lk 1:30;
Jn 6:20), speaks to you in a special way one day. Or perhaps
you are struck by the cry of the blind beggar in the gospel of
Luke, "Lord, please let me see" (Lk 18:41). Such prayer may
tell us things about our longings and needs, about our relationship with God. It may provide us with food for reflection
or conversation with a spiritual director. But we have to be
careful with it. It is too easy to superstitiously expect the Bible
to provide us with simple answers to the complex dilemmas
of our lives. More frequently scripture unlocks the big questions, questions that we try to answer with our lives.

Unpacking the Tradition

Of course, the work of handing down the faith of the
apostles did not cease with the production of the New
Testament. The faith had to be handed down, and to grow
and develop as it was. The transmission of that faith over the

centuries, and the evidence of its growth and change, is what we call "tradition." Unfortunately, like discipline, tradition is a frequent casualty of distorted images—images of customs we repeat without knowing why, of unreasonable old rules and regulations, of cultural norms of ages gone by that no longer seem to fit in our own time. These are authentic manifestations of tradition, to be sure, but not all of it is "moldy oldies"; properly understood, much of it remains valuable to us today.

Looked upon as a whole, tradition is a majestic entity, the collected wisdom of those who have gone before us in faith. Much of it is the timeless witness of brilliant people of the past—the theological clarity of the Cappodocian Fathers, the poetic imagery of God of Hildegard of Bingen, the mystical insights of St. John of the Cross, the passion for justice of Dorothy Day. It is rich and varied, often containing the teachings of both sides of an issue. Its customs, liturgies, theologies, mysticism, heroes, and heroines (saints!) cut through and speak to us in our time and place from historical circumstances remote to us.

That historical remoteness, however, makes tradition hard to fathom at times. As with any story or piece of writing (including the scriptures), our Catholic traditions come with the historical baggage of their era. If we approach them without a sense of history and without some reference to the circumstances that produced them, we run the risk of misunderstanding. A modern reader poring over *The Interior Castle* of Teresa of Avila will find Teresa's self-deprecation and desire for penance and poverty shocking and bizarre. But take into consideration the literary style of the time and realize that Teresa is in the middle of reforming her lax and self-satisfied religious order, and her reactions don't seem quite so extreme. So it is with all of the "giants" of our tradition. To drink them in without knowing the situation they faced leads us to a gullible and naive acceptance of all they say. This is a species of Catholic fundamentalism, and it is not helpful on the road of faith.

Tradition, properly understood, is helpful. The job of the contemporary person of faith is to "unpack" the tradition a little, to wade through the different attitudes of the time, perhaps by taking in a book *about* the spiritual giant in question rather than (or before) the text itself. At times this investigation will require great effort. Surprisingly, much of the time it does not. There are all kinds of modern interpreters and commentators around to help us unpack the tradition—theologians, teachers, spiritual directors, historians. With their help, it gets easier. In any case, we need our traditions as maps on the road of faith. Learning the lessons of the past has considerable advantage over learning everything by our own mistakes.

Community: The Living Tradition in Progress

We know that Christian tradition did not drop from heaven in written form. The wisdom of the past was once the wisdom of the present. If this is true, then today we are creating the tradition of tomorrow. We do it just as the early Christians did when, with the inspiration of the Holy Spirit, they celebrated the first Christian gatherings and formed the writings of the New Testament. We too benefit from the inspiration of the Holy Spirit. But like the early Christians, we must take St. Paul's advice and "test everything" (1 Thes 5:21). We test our wisdom by placing it before the community.

The community is the repository of wisdom. As we have already stated, there is no such thing as an individualist Christian. It is the nature of human beings to long for community, and we bring together our wisdom there. Therefore, we go to the community to be educated in our faith. We go to gather information to make conscientious moral choices. We go to have our most important decisions tested according to the collective wisdom. That is why we send our children to religious education classes, why we listen to our church leaders' teachings on topics of moral controversy, why we are married and ordained (in a public ceremony) only after a preparation process created by the community.

There are many reasons why the community is the repository of Christian wisdom and not an individual. Some are obvious, such as protection against one person's tyrannical ambitions or mental instability. Others are more subtle, such as the "synergistic property" of a community; that is, the efforts of the whole turn out better than the sum of the individual parts. In a group, people achieve better things than they do by themselves, for the ideas and works of individuals build on one another in a frenzy of creativity and wisdom. Hasn't everyone had the experience of being in a group where the energy of group interaction created a better product than anyone could have created by herself or himself?

A final word ought to be said about community. Not every group that comes together is a community. Communities require diversity, openness to new members, and a commitment both to one another and to the outside world. Exclusive groups that set themselves against the world, that insulate members from other people, that alienate and ostracize those who choose to leave—these groups are not communities, they are cults. Communities break open our perspective; they do not narrow it down.

There is, of course, infinitely more to say about community. Suffice it to say that there are some excellent books to read on the topic. *Habits of the Heart* and *The Good Society* by Robert Bellah and his associates are excellent works on community in the United States; *Community and Growth* by Jean Vanier is one of the premier works on spiritual communities (Vanier founded the L'Arche communities that work with the developmentally disabled all over the world); and Dick

Westley's *Redemptive Intimacy* is a down-to-earth discussion of faith, church, and relationship.

Scripture, Tradition, Community: Practical Considerations

In the previous chapter, we talked about discipline as an essential supply on the road of faith, a kind of "spiritual motor oil." The spiritual giants of our Christian tradition agree that it is particularly important to take a disciplined approach to the key areas of scripture, tradition, and community. Growing in faith really requires a basic commitment to things like spiritual reading and communal practice.

Spiritual reading includes both Bible and tradition. Many suggest reading at least twenty minutes a day. When reading Scripture, it's always helpful to peek into some kind of commentary as well. As for the tradition, many find it more agreeable to begin in the present, because recent authors seem more accessible. Besides, they nearly always incorporate the insights of people gone by. As for where to start, it is best to check in with someone who knows you and who is conversant with books by good authors. A spiritual director or clergyperson may be helpful. When all else fails, check the appendix of this book. Gathered there are works recommended by the spiritual directors of insight and repute that I know.

The discipline of communal practice is also key. We need the support and challenge of other believers. That usually translates to some type of regular communal worship. We need to break open the scriptures together and celebrate our unity in Christ at the eucharistic table. Once people have made a serious commitment to the spiritual journey, they often find it is not enough to pray to God on their own. Many seekers find they want to have some kind of faith-sharing community as well, and many parishes today are forming these.

Some choose a small prayer group or a retreat group; others go for some other smaller community committed to the work of uncovering the meaning of the gospel in our lives together. The long and the short of it is that together we can guard against each other's faults and multiply our strengths.

The Spiritual Companion

Part of the responsibility of any community of faith is to provide for the continuing spiritual growth of its members. Thus, the community chooses a number of leaders it deems "spiritual friends," companion-guides for the road of faith. Seekers, especially in times of great question and vulnerability, ask for their help along the way. In a way this makes sense. Every art and trade is taught by apprenticeship; the art of spirituality is no exception. Naturally, that does not mean that the apprentice copies every move the mentor makes. Nor does it mean that the mentor tells the apprentice what to do. It merely means that each of us needs a person of greater experience to help us along the way—to comfort us, to challenge us, to pass on to us the lessons of his or her past. The spiritual companion relationship is a way to keep us from having to learn everything from our own mistakes. That person can be a "giver of shortcuts" and most especially a "reality check" for our individual ways of looking at the world.

The spiritual guide is sometimes a difficult concept for our individualistic society to embrace, so I think it appropriate to mention one last point. We can always say "no" to a spiritual director or guide's suggestion. We can always disagree with what that person has to say. We are not talking about a military-style relationship. Spiritual directors and companions are not generals, providing orders for our every move. They are the bearers of experience. If a guide seems to have a good judgment and a lot of insight into reality, it would be wise to consider his or her advice carefully before making a decision. Of course, wise people have been wrong many times in history. But more often they have been right.

Friendship

The spiritual benefits of good, mature friendship are too many to be counted. Friends who share faith support each other in the journey of life. They care for each other when the chips are down and rejoice together when times are joyful. True friends are not afraid to challenge each other and to seek each other out as a "reality check." Through companionship, empathy, and commitment, they build each other up across both the potholes and the smooth highways of life. They exchange ideas and collaborate on tasks. In all of this they stand side by side, for real friendship is a relationship of mutuality and equality. This is not to say that everything that friends do for each other comes out balanced on some kind of relational ledger sheet. Generosity and creativity enter into friendship so that each member gets more out of it than she puts into it.

Let's not be naive about friendship, however. It requires hard work, good interpersonal skills, and a certain degree of vulnerability. Many people avoid true friendship out of laziness, frustration, or fear. Fear probably puts off the largest number of people. If people come to know me as friend, to know my personality, my thoughts and my feelings, they might use such things against me. Indeed, this does happen. Even Jesus was not immune to being betrayed by a friend.

Yet most people find true friendship worth the risk. Moreover, one can use good judgment in choosing friends. Some of us go through our lives cultivating relationships with people that drag us down instead of building us up. We cannot afford such adventures in insecurity and vindictiveness.

We had best take care to choose friends in whose presence we become better people, not worse!

Once we choose friends, there is the task of maintaining friendship. One of the key issues here is that of "personal boundaries." Boundaries have to do with the emotional distance that we maintain between us and other people. Psychologists today talk about the need for *strong* yet *permeable* personal boundaries in relationships.

For some people, the difficulty involves the "strong" part. These folks too easily collapse themselves into pleasing other people, losing track of their own wishes, desires, and needs. This is stereotypically what women do, but men are not immune either. When I was a teenager, I would only be interested in a girl if I knew that she was interested in me. It was her desire that was important, not mine. I didn't even know what I wanted. Then I inevitably ended up trying to rescue these girls from whatever problems they had. Of course, I wasn't giving them the space to seek their own solutions as we all must. Yes, love involves self-giving, but you have to have a self to give!

On the other hand, there are those people (stereotypically men) who have trouble with the "permeable" part. It is difficult for them to share, to allow friends in close, to "let people in." Have you ever known someone (or been the one) who's got everything bottled up inside, who is convinced she's got to hold it all together on her own? Have you wondered why men are flocking to meetings like Promise Keepers and going out into the woods to beat drums? It's a chance to go to a sacred place to let the boundaries slip a little and share some hopes and fears with their friends.

Although friendship is surely to be enjoyed for its own sake, Christians also see it as "the school of love." In other words, in the life of a friendship, we discover how to navigate the joys and difficulties of relationship. We learn when to come close and when to give space. We learn how to "just be there" when there is nothing left to say. Over the long term, friendship painfully teaches us the difference between fighting fair and fighting unfair. Through our friends we learn who we are and who they are. Thus, friendship is the basis of romantic love. It is the goal of parent-child relationships after children grow up. Through its ups and downs, it teaches us to truly commit beyond ourselves.

Nourishing us on the road of faith, friendship instructs us about the kingdom of God. In the gospel of John, Jesus says, "This is my commandment: that you love one another as I have loved you.... I do not call you servants any longer, for the servant does not know what the master is doing; but I have called you friends, because I have made known to you everything that I have heard from my Father" (Jn 15:12,15). The lifelong task of a disciple is to become a true friend of Jesus Christ. We discover this friendship, not by feeling "warm fuzzies" for him in our hearts, but by learning to live and love as he did.

Prayer—Cellular Phone to the Most High?

Although we do not "bring God along" on our spiritual journey, God remains our most important companion. All our relationships with people eventually lead us to relationship with God. As some have put it, we fall in love throughout our lives that we might finally fall in love with God.

We say that God is Trinity, three persons in one God. Perhaps the most important thing we learn from this dogma is that our God is a God that operates in relationship. The Father, Son, and Holy Spirit remain always in relationship with each other and with us. As St. Paul says, "I am convinced that neither death, nor life, nor angels, nor rulers, nor things present, nor things to come...nor anything else in all creation, will be able to separate us from the love of God in Christ Jesus our

Lord" (Rom 8:38–39). In no way initiated by us, our relationship with God is what makes the difference in our lives, car-
rying us through the difficult times, challenging us in times of
complacency, and granting us the necessary perspective to
see beyond all the complex and frightening elements of our
lives, even our death.

I begin our discussion of prayer with this insight because
the temptation is always to imagine that prayer begins from
our end. It does not! God is always in communication with us,
beginning with Creation and culminating in the life, death,
and resurrection of Christ. Any discussion of prayer must
begin with an understanding that communication with God is
first a matter of *listening*. Our role is to keep the lines of communication open. From the start this means awareness, it
means always seeking to find out what God is saying to us in
our lives. It also means a discipline of prayer. When we do not
set aside a regular time to be attuned to God's voice in our
lives, it is all too easy to become permanently distracted, spiritually asleep.

Our prayer doesn't always have to occur in the same manner, however. As children, many of us had a certain approach
to prayer drilled into us. You say these prayers (rosary,
Angelus, Our Father, whatever) so many times a day and you
do not deviate! If we persist in this approach to prayer in
adulthood, it will inevitably become a dry duty. Why not
allow creativity and spontaneity to creep into our prayer life?
It is important every now and then to allow new images of
God to take the place of old ones that die away. Our faith
changes as we grow throughout our lives. We sometimes
think that because we cannot pray as we used to, we have lost
our faith. But this is not so. It is only that God is challenging
us to grow to a new and different level of prayerful intimacy.
In the final analysis, all of our thoughts and images concerning God are not God. Our whole life is reaching toward the
unknowable God. If we do not allow our prayer to change

and grow, we will find ourselves chanting before some idol instead of the Holy Divine Mystery.

But *practically* speaking, how do we pray? Many people complain that they do not know where to start. The place to start is squarely within our experience. How is it that I find God in my life? Some find God in walks in nature, others through music and chant. We have already alluded to the use of the imagination in listening to God. The mystic tradition speaks of the prayer of silence, often called meditation or centering prayer, although this prayer is difficult for many of us. However we choose to pray, it must remain connected to our experience. The temptation is to propel ourselves into the cosmic stratosphere. We start to pray from where we *want to be* instead of from where we are. Through the centuries, Christian tradition has maintained that prayer is a relationship with God from *where we are*. Prayer does not lift us into some "spiritual" realm where we have direct access to God. It helps us to find the ways in which God's presence is mediated to us in our daily life.

We have said that prayer is a relationship. As such, it involves difficulties and struggles just as all relationships do. We will become angry with God, perhaps even to the point of screaming. We need not fear this; nonviolent anger is a part of all healthy relationships. We may find ourselves in dry periods when God seems far away. This too is a normal part of the relationship. And there are the false images of God that are nearly impossible to get out of our heads. These will be relinquished over time. Prayer is not a reason for anxiety or tight control. Rather, prayer is a matter of listening, a matter of letting go.

Much has been written and said about prayer in our tradition; far be it from me to repeat it all here. There are several volumes on prayer worthy of consideration listed in the appendix. A spiritual director is nearly always a good place to go when it comes to learning how to pray.

A final note: The test of prayer is not good feelings, calmness, or the amount of time spent in quiet meditation. The test of prayer is love. We know we are truly open in our prayer if God is transforming us into more loving people.

The Unwelcome Companion—Suffering

Now comes the most unwelcome of spiritual companions—suffering. If we're to image it as a companion, then it would probably be the backseat driver, the person in line at the store who can't stop talking, the burr in my shoe, the insect trapped within a car. However we describe it, we do not desire it, and yet it will always be with us.

For years people have been telling me that suffering was "redemptive." I resisted the notion for just as long. How can pain and hurt help us become closer to God? More often than not, this idea left me with the feeling that somehow God was a sadist, an unhappy individual who wanted us all to suffer for God's own gratification. As I grew in my understanding of God, however, it became quite clear that this was impossible. So I reached again to understand the purpose of suffering.

In some ways, I never found it. This should not surprise me or anyone else. Twenty-five hundred years ago, the author of the book of Job posed the question of suffering, and the best he (or perhaps she, no one knows) could do was to affirm the value of faith in the face of suffering. What, for example, are we to say of the horrendous sufferings human evil has visited on our own century—the Holocaust, the scandalous prevalence of hunger and poverty in the world, the mass murders in Stalinist Russia, the death squads in El Salvador, the genocide in Rwanda? Are we to say that God willed it or even allowed it to happen? No one would want any part of a God who did! Such suffering is strictly the result of terrible and malicious deeds by human beings. Yet even if we put aside the issue of human evil, what of suffering for which there is no one to blame? What of natural disasters, terminal illness, accidents, and the sting of grief over a lost loved one? All we can say in the face of such things is that suffering exists, and part of the job of faith is to come to terms with it.

Christianity looks at suffering and gives us the Cross of Christ. Traditionally, we have thought about the Cross as that which washes away our sins. Unfortunately, this outlook sometimes leads to the idea that God is angry and must be appeased with the human sacrifice of his son. Surely this is not the God we believe in! Seen from another angle, the Cross becomes instead the sign that God's love is stronger than even death, for after death on the cross came resurrection. It affirms that God does not abandon us, even and especially in times of great suffering. It brings us back to the lesson of Job—the only response to suffering is trust in God. There may even be lessons and meanings in the suffering. This is not to say that God wills it, but only that God can write straight even with the most crooked of lines.

What kind of lessons can pain teach us? It has taught persistence, toughness, and endurance. People find themselves able to go the extra mile for God because of it. It teaches compassion. When I see that my own wounds are also the wounds of others, I am capable of helping others to heal. Suffering reminds us that we are not in full control of our lives. It is the irrefutable sign of our limitations. An older woman hobbling painfully across a courtyard the other day asked for my arm to help her walk. When I gave it, she looked at me and said, "As you get older, you get less inhibited about asking other people for help." Hers is a good example. In the best situations, the painful experience of our limitations bids us recognize our need for each other and our need for God.

Of course, such lessons do not apply to all pain and suffering, and ultimately we do not know why we must suffer as we do. What we do know is that it is a part of life. When it is placed before us, we must confront it so that we might learn and grow. Whatever happens, the truth of Job remains—God is with us.

> Then Job answered the Lord and said,
> "I know that you can do all things,
>   and that no purpose of yours can be hindered.
> I have dealt with great things that I do not understand;
>   things too wonderful for me, which I cannot know.
> I had heard of you by word of mouth,
>   but now my eye has seen you."
>
> (Jb 42:1–5)

Our compassionate God, rich in mercy, suffers with us and offers us comfort, learning, and help.

Chapter Ten: ACCOUTREMENTS OF A MATURE FAITH

Throughout this book, we have talked about finding God's presence in every part of our lives. In the words of St. Monica, "There is no place that is far from God." As God enters into each part of our experience, we respond to our loving Creator. In other words, we try to "get it together" with God in our whole lives. This is appropriate talk for young adults, for our developmental task at hand is to discover ourselves in growth and development, to find out and become more fully who we are. For us particularly then, the journey of faith is one of balance and integration. We attempt to orient our whole selves—body and mind, heart and spirit—to good, to love, to God. This demands that we pay attention to the whole of our lives, seeking to find health, wholeness, and love there. We attend to our physical health, gift of God that it is. We attend to our psychological and mental well-being and growth. We look to the social sphere, ensuring supportive and challenging contact with other people that leads to better lives for all of us. Ultimately, our aim is participating in God's transformation of the world into the reign of God, but part of that aim is ensuring that every part of us and everyone else is well maintained.

Health and Well-Being

Though it was never lost, the idea of good physical health as an element of spiritual growth was hidden from view for many of the Christian centuries. Instead of celebrating the body as the seed of future resurrection (1 Cor 15:37), we subscribed to a dualistic view of the world, dividing reality into the categories of "material" and "spiritual." The material was the lower realm, full of dirt and plants and animals and sex and sin (the latter two usually made equivalent). The higher plane was the spiritual, where there were God and angels and nice, antiseptic things like that. Human beings, unfortunate schizophrenics that we are, found ourselves split between the two levels. The trick, then, was to elevate ourselves above the material plane to the spiritual plane. In other words, get over your body and live a "spiritual" life! The problems with this system are obvious—God's creation gets a bad rap; sex becomes an evil act even under the most positive circumstances; we end up neglecting and abusing our bodies in our hurry to become like the angels.

The more holistic spirituality that we observe today (and have always observed in the best moments of our tradition) will have none of this. Creation is unequivocally good; God does not create garbage. Spiritual growth does not come by bypassing our bodies, but by allowing God to work through our whole selves. In the words of St. Irenaeus, "The glory of God is the human person fully alive." This includes all of us, especially our bodies. If we are to be effective signs of God's presence in the world, we have to take care of ourselves. So things like exercise, rest, diet, and attitude become more than just good habits. They become building blocks for the reign of God.

Our contemporary environment seems to be becoming more and more health conscious. We focus a lot of attention on what "modern medicine" has done for us. There are health clubs all over the place. Every item in the supermarket has the fat content marked on the back. We should be getting healthier, but we're not. Our consumer culture demands "quick fixes," but health is a long-term project. We go on binges of taking care of ourselves, but I wonder whether most of us really follow through for the long run. Take sleep. How many of us get the eight hours of sleep every night that doctors recommend? Catching up on the weekends won't cut it. Yet most of us don't even approach the necessary amount. Sleep ends up being very low on our priority list. My friend Frank sarcastically notes our approach to sleep when he says, "Sleep? You'll have plenty of time to sleep when you're dead."

These patterns of denial have to stop. Taking care of ourselves means establishing patterns of adequate sleep, regular exercise (cardiovascular at least three times a week), and a balanced diet. I don't know about you, but about the time someone says this to me, I groan with dread. I have visions of giving up everything that is fun and filling my life with boredom. Not so. Not all of a proper diet tastes bad. Everyone likes some kind of exercise, whether it be a sport or hiking or bicycling or whatever. Even sleep has its satisfactions. Taking pleasure in these activities of personal maintenance is a challenge at times, but not an insurmountable one. If uncoordinated people like me can find pleasure in exercise, anyone can!

A final note about mental health. This is a complex area, but as with physical health, there are some basic truths to attend to here. A good chunk of mental health is attitude. Everyone loves to complain, but in the long term excessive negative thoughts drag us down. Without being falsely optimistic, the maintenance of a positive attitude does a lot for our personal well-being. (Also, it keeps other people from avoiding us!) This brings us to another point about mental health. Regular conversation with those with whom we are close gives us a boost on the road to happiness. We get a chance to relate not only the events of our lives but our feelings about them as well. And keeping our minds active is another element of mental health. While occasional "vegging" can be relaxing, too much time in the land of the couch potatoes makes us all dull boys and girls.

Rest Stops

Returning to our road trip metaphor, something can be said about the pace of our spiritual travels. After all, sometimes when we take to the road, we go nonstop. We travel three hundred miles in six hours and pull off the highway only once for gasoline. Other times, we take a more leisurely pace, making rest stops along the way—to eat, to stretch our legs, or perhaps just to take a closer look at a view we glimpsed from the road.

Along the road of our life journeys, we use both of these traveling styles, depending on a hundred different characteristics of a given situation. The difficulty erupts when our lives are too unbalanced in the direction of nonstop travel. We have deadlines to meet, overtime to work, and commitments to keep, so we just don't stop. We spend all our time doing things (or at least worrying about them), and those vital rest stops are missing from our lives. Yet the rest stops are what teach us to *be,* to recognize that our worth comes from *who we are* and not from what we *do.* Now I realize that sometimes we have no choice; we have to work without pause. But if nonstop has become a lifestyle rather than an occasional rush, we need to seriously rethink our perspective. The long-term prospects for health are not good. Sooner or later, we will run out of gas. We require those rest stops to re-energize, to renew our spirits, to make contact with God and the basics of being human.

Play and Recreation

Taking time out for play is absolutely essential to the spiritual life! Play is an eruption of creativity, spontaneity, and fun. It is allowing the child within each of us to emerge and rejoice; it is a "letting go." If we find ourselves pondering, "Am I playing?" then certainly we are not. Play allows us to let go, be creative, and have a good time; it is rejuvenating and energizing; we walk away from it excited about life.

It ought to be easy to play, right? Only the most fanatical workaholic would dismiss play as frivolous and childish (of course, it *is* frivolous and childish—that's the point). The problem has more to do with knowing *how* to play than with a willingness to do so. Even as young adults, we have already grown up too much—we've forgotten how to play. We know how to engage in games and sports, but that is more recreation than play. We also know how to be entertained. Our society loves entertainment, loves television and the movies; but entertainment is not play, because it is passive. Play requires participation. You have to *be there* to play. To play we need to get creative, to recall a childlike sense of wonder, to engage people and activities without a productive purpose in mind. Play is its own goal, and it always results in the feeling that we are celebrating life.

On the other hand, we might remember that certain activities that are seldom identified with having fun can be playful. Intellectual study can actually be playful if it activates that curious, wonder-filled kid inside us. Our work might be play if we get lost in creative and spontaneous moments. Worship can even be play; in fact, that's the way it was originally designed (though you would never know it visiting some "zombie churches"). In worship, as in creative goofing off, the idea is to lose our self-consciousness and get caught up in the joy of being alive. Celebrating being alive is worshipping the Author of Life. Acknowledging this, a spiritual director of mine noted that the closest thing to prayer among other human activities is play.

Distinct from play theoretically, though not always in practice, is recreation. Recreation is regular engagement in certain activities that we enjoy by virtue of our background or personal likes. We recreate by participating in sports, by working on hobbies, by reading a favorite type of literature. Some may be more partial to researching a topic near and dear to their hearts or to practicing a musical instrument. Recreation depends on what we like to do. Recreation is a part of the balanced spiritual diet. It rounds us out, gives us a healthy distraction, and trains us in a set of skills different from those required for our chief tasks in life.

Solitude

Spiritual Faux Pas: Continually surrounding myself with people and activities to avoid some deeper issue with which I do not want to struggle.

People we know accompany us throughout most of our life journeys. Activities and tasks familiar to us require most of our time. This is normal life, and no one is disputing the goodness of that. But there also comes a time to remove oneself from those normal circumstances and travel a bit of that road of faith alone. We need to go away to a quiet (or at least quieter) place by ourselves and breathe deeply, think, reflect, pray, and listen to what is being said to us in the deepest parts of our being. It calms us and gives us some welcome internal quiet to balance off the chaos of life.

It must be said, however, that solitude will not always calm us; at times it will bring up difficult questions and problems, unresolved inner conflicts. Anyone who has really entered into a silent retreat will attest to this. But part of what we seek from solitude is a safe place where, with God close by, we can face the unresolved conflicts and issues in our lives. These are the mysterious parts of our lives that are both wounds and strengths—strained parental relationships, fears of abandonment, buried hurts and betrayals, feelings of worthlessness, questions and fears about our sexuality. Solitude reminds us that the skeletons in our psychological closets (we all have them) will not go away because we ignore, avoid, or deny them. They will drag us down until we choose to deal with them. When we do decide to deal with them, over time something magical happens. Wounds become strengths. God transforms our deepest fears and resentments to wells of compassion and endurance that allow us to share our vulnerability with other people. Solitude is a key element of this process that also involves much faith and sometimes outside professional help.

A last word about solitude: Solitude and loneliness are not the same thing. Solitude is aloneness intentionally cultivated for good. Loneliness is a feeling that often creeps up on us, whether we are alone or with others. When our personal needs for companionship are not being met, loneliness results. We long to have some other person come and take care of us. Loneliness is a powerful force in our lives. It calls us to seek companionship. But sometimes it is so severe that we seek company uncritically; we try to accelerate relationships before their time. Loneliness is ultimately good, for it sends us into the company of other human beings. Still, we have to realize that relationships have their own speed, their own times and seasons. Some loneliness is part of the human condition, and all of us have to learn to deal with it. Chronic and severe loneliness, however, is a different matter. It may mean that some counseling or professional psychological help is needed.

Belonging

We spent the whole previous chapter commenting on the essential need for community of human beings. Its roots are in an emotional need we all have deeply ingrained in us—the need to *belong*. Its power manifests itself in the terrible loss we feel when we are rejected by a group of people (family, friends, faith community). Historically, banishment functioned well as a punishment because human beings found it so intolerable to be tossed out of their basic groupings. In contemporary life, the result of this need is that most of us belong to all kinds of groups. The initial grouping is family, but our sense of belonging grows from there. We are socialized into ethnic groups, classes at school, groups of friends, social clubs, sports teams, religious communities, and so forth.

For those who see life as a faith journey, some kind of religious affiliation is important. We long not only for the grand scale belonging of a large church community, but for the intimacy of a smaller faith-sharing community as well. Yet in our task-oriented society, too often small faith communities become groups for "doing" something, whether it be liturgy planning, community service, or education. We require and want to have such groups, but another type of group is also important. According to the best wisdom of spiritual tradition, *being* is actually more important than *doing*. Our sense of worth is based on who we are (children of God) more than what we do. Thus, we need faith-sharing groups, where the point is not organizing or activity, but being with each other. We share our experiences of life and seek together to find the hand of God in them. A sense of mutual support and bonding develops that makes our faith exciting and worthwhile.

For many people, immediate and extended family satisfy most belonging needs throughout life. But families "of generation" have their limitations, especially in an individualist, mobile society where divorce and other break-ups of the family are common. Family is important for those who have it and benefit by it; but alternative communities, "families of choice," must be found for those who do not.

The Repair Shop

Having everything we need on our road of faith, sharing the journey with God and good companions, keeping a sense of healthy balance and integration can all come to naught on our road trip if we break down. And the fact is, despite the best of precautions, we *do* break down. When this happens, we need outside help. The crisis might be physical, mental, emotional, or spiritual. When the breakdown is physical, we usually know what to do visit our doctor or other health professional. In the emotional or mental realm, things get fuzzier. For what problems should I seek the help of a counselor or therapist, and when should I do it? I think at heart we really know, though we may try to procrastinate or deny it. We know when an issue (like excessive anger or family alcoholism) troubles us enough that "growth counseling" is in order. We know when our lives spin sufficiently out of control that we need the assistance of a psychologist to put it all back together. And we know when the problem reaches crisis proportions, such as with clinical depression or hallucinations, that our good mental health requires a psychiatrist's counsel.

Apart from this question of knowing, many people resist help in matters of the mind and heart. They feel it a sign of weakness or a violation of good behavior ("You don't air your dirty laundry in front of strangers"). When the need is serious enough, however, we have to let go of such objections for our own good. Everyone has problems. One out of every three people experiences severe depression in his or her life. Only extreme individualists think they can always handle everything on their own. The important thing is to be open to seeking help when we need it.

For modern people, the "spiritual breakdown" or *crisis of faith* is even more confusing than emotional difficulties. There is an idea afoot that faith is a one-time gift. If it changes or if I experience doubts or a lack of clarity, then I have lost it. As has been said already, this is far from the truth! Doubts and unclarity usually point to dramatic spiritual growth underway. Anger with God and an inability to pray probably indicate the same thing. Rather than signaling the end of our faith life, they indicate a new development in it. Sometimes these spiritual crises just erupt out of nowhere. Other times, a medical or psychological problem spurs a faith crisis. Deep depression, addiction, grief over the death of someone close—such things often lead people to a crisis of faith. Suddenly, all that was clear about God and about life's meaning becomes unclear.

Whatever the crisis, God is at work! But most of us need help to discover God's mysterious purposes (and to get us through). Looking to the Christian community, we seek those "in the know," people whose faith has survived and flourished through life's hardships, people who have meditated on God's work in their lives and have words to speak about it. We draw from the wisdom of spiritual directors and pastors, of confessors and fellow parishioners whom we respect and trust.

Whatever the crisis—whether medical, psychological, or spiritual—professional help remains a boon to us. Still, we cannot afford to be uncritical about it. There are bad doctors, counselors, spiritual directors, priests, and ministers out there. It pays to be reflective and to ask periodically, "Is this person's assistance making things better or not? Does he or she really have something to offer me?" Furthermore, if helping professionals begin to cross personal boundaries and seek intimacy in inappropriate ways, we must acknowledge that they thereby abuse their power, and we need to discontinue their services. Lastly, we need to remember that the point of seeking professional help is to get us back to coping on our own. Other people cannot solve our problems for us, but they can use their skills to train us in solving our difficulties for ourselves.

Chapter Eleven: DISCERNMENT— MAPPING MY ROAD OF FAITH

Truly you have formed my inmost being;
    you knit me in my mother's womb.
I give you thanks that I am fearfully, wonderfully made;
    wonderful are your works.
My soul also you knew full well;
    nor was my frame unknown to you
When I was made in secret,
    when I was fashioned in the depths of the earth.
Your eyes have seen my actions;
    in your book they are all written;
    my days were limited before one of them existed.
How weighty are your designs, O God;
    how vast the sum of them!
Were I to count them, they would outnumber the sands;
    did I reach the end of them, I should still be with you.
                    (Psalm 139:13–18)

God has fashioned each of us uniquely. No two lives are exactly the same, so each of us has a unique destiny. There is much spiritual wisdom in the world, to be sure, but it applies slightly differently in each person's life. Therefore we need *discernment,* the lifelong process of "uncovering the way as we go." It is based on the idea that the Holy Spirit is always with us in this life, giving guidance and empowering us to go forward. But our spiritual tradition also recognizes that the Spirit does not generally upset the balance of nature by giving us extraordinary signs. Few human beings have seen their whole future written in bold letters in the sky. The Spirit makes her ways known to us in the ordinary signs of everyday life. Learning to read these signs and detect in them the promptings of God is what we mean by discernment. Uncovering these promptings gives us essential input to navigate our way on the road of faith.

Paying Attention to the Signs

Discernment begins with attention to the signs of our times. The Spirit places all kinds of clues, signals, and directional keys in our lives. We cannot, however, give our attention to every piece of information that crosses our path. Instead, we learn to give our attention to the right types of cues as best we can.

In Ordinary Places

It is too easy to succumb to the temptation to look for miraculous or at least unusual signs from on high. I may anxiously read about the messages of Mary in Medjugorje or perhaps superstitiously conclude that God wants me to be an airline pilot because while praying for career guidance I heard Elton John's song "Take Me to the Pilot." The truth is that the Spirit speaks more through the ordinary than the extraordinary. I do not mean to say that exotic divine intervention is impossible; it's just that excessive attention to these more remote occurrences takes the everyday Post-its from the Holy Ghost out of focus. Ordinary life provides all the input we need for discerning the movement of the Spirit in our lives. Looking for extraordinary signs is a waste of time.

In Common Sense

Corollary to this comes the idea that the Spirit speaks through common sense and tends toward the pragmatic. This flies in the face of the stereotype of the so-called spiritual person who has his head in the clouds. Indeed, I will witness to this error. This reformed "space cadet" found himself in much better spiritual shape once others had called him back to earth for an intensive training session in paying attention to the world around him. Common sense depends on collecting data and doing pragmatic, intuitive analysis. One can be an excellent analyst but a terrible data collector, as I was. On the other hand, one can be a wonderful data collector who never applies himself or herself to analysis. We need to do both— pay attention to the details of life, and then make sure that we are willing to put our minds to work on them.

In the Outside World

Where does one look for the signs of the Spirit? First, we might distinguish between external and internal signs. For the external ones, we look to our situation in life. They come from our environment, from chains of events that surround us, from people in our lives. Some of them are more obvious than others. For example, if I have demonstrated a stunning talent in science, I should probably major in one of the sciences. If a young woman's boyfriend abuses her, God would surely be calling on her to leave him. But most signs are not written in bold that way, and we have to train ourselves to attend to them. A friend of mine was ready to apply for graduate school. I have it on good authority that no stranger approached him in the hall and said mysteriously, "Go to Carnegie-Mellon." If a stranger had, he certainly wouldn't have trusted him. Instead, he talked to his wife about where they would want to live, looked at a lot of literature in his field, asked the opinions of some professors he respected, and surveyed the preferences of companies he would like to work for. The signs were there, but he had to go looking for them.

Whether they be obvious or not, the first signs of the Spirit's guidance that we tend to notice occur in and through other people. Sometimes it's a deliberate search. An acquaintance of mine told me he felt that God was calling him to join a church, to become part of a faith community. He immediately began visiting the churches of friends whose faith he admired, looking for the place that fit him. At other times the sign comes quite unsought and unexpectedly. My mother has a friend who used to be a hairstylist, quite content in her job. One day as she and a customer were talking, her client said to her, "Have you ever thought about being a counselor or social worker or something? You'd be good at it." She had never thought about it, but after that conversation, she could not stop thinking about it. She eventually got her degree and started practicing.

Beyond other people, our environment gives us all kinds of signs of God's will for us. It was Dorothy Day's awareness of the homelessness and poverty around her in New York City that eventually led her to found the Catholic Worker movement. Noting the depletion of the ozone layer has led many a scientist to begin focusing studies on it. Seeing the economic opportunities down South led my great-grandfather to move his family there in the 1920s. These were all signs in the environment.

Chains of events also give us signals of God's work in our lives, especially when there seems to be a convergence of events. The same week a friend found himself wearing down from his long commute, a passerby asked him if he wanted to sell his house. It set my friend to thinking about moving. As a young soldier, the German theologian Johann Metz was called away from his unit to deliver a message. When he returned, every person in his unit was dead. Later, as he began a career in theology, that powerful incident (among others) convinced him to look into the problem of human evil.

Of course, not every external sign is authentic, worthy of being followed. Ways to test such signs will be discussed below. However, the critical issue here is that God is always trying to tell us something; and the Spirit of God writes these messages into the fabric, events, and people of our world. By questioning and paying close attention, we may learn a thing or two about the way to go.

The Internal Signs

"The source of all true progress consists in increased attention and fidelity to the action of the Holy Spirit in the soul." So said Isaac Hecker, an American Catholic spiritual thinker of the last century. Hecker took very seriously Jesus' promise that the Spirit would always dwell in our hearts. Thus, just as we look for signs of the Spirit's guidance outside of ourselves, so we need to peruse the internal signs of the Spirit when we discern. Contemporary Christian theology backs up this assertion, for it acknowledges human experience as the window through which we know God. We could experience nothing without the workings of our mind and heart; they are the channels for signs of God's guidance. There are at least three internal avenues to consider: thinking (or reflection), feeling, and intuition. The giants of the spiritual life suggest that discernment requires consideration of all three.

The reflecting end of this has already entered into the discussion. The best discernment requires analysis. I say that I want to marry you because we are compatible. Why do I say that? Because we never fight? If so, do we not fight because we agree all the time or because we both are unable to deal with conflict? Good discernment requires that we use our brains. It is easy to glaze over facts, especially if emotions or intuition are voting wholeheartedly for a particular course of action. But poorly reasoned discernment makes for mistaken decisions. On the other hand, of course, discernment that relies completely and only on analysis doesn't cut the mustard either (though it is often the way that we men make our big decisions). Rejecting the emotions and intuition can bring about a "headiness" or rationalization in which the result of discernment makes perfect sense but does not satisfy human needs. It becomes disconnected from our life experience. It could even be cold or cruel.

Spiritual Faux Pas: Making all my big decisions based on how I feel.

Emotions are more complicated to deal with than thinking. We often say things about "trusting your heart" and "doing what feels right," but emotions are a tricky business. If I am a passionate person (and I am), I have to be careful that my emotions do not rule my life. I need to make sure my mind is working in tandem with my heart in discerning.

Emotions are a gift from God. They provide flavor for life, excitement, and drama. They keep us from becoming bored with life's routine. We cannot totally control them. Anger, fear, joy, and frustration will strike when they wish, and denying their presence will not banish them. They will creep back up from the subconscious. What I *can* control is how I express my emotions. I can also decide whether or not they affect my decisions.

Being able to read our emotions is an important part of discernment. The Spirit may be speaking through our feelings. A sense of indignation at an injustice may lead me to do something about it. Perhaps a long-standing anger with God is a sign that I need to go back and mourn someone who died years ago. Excitement that erupts when I am doing my job probably indicates that this is a good job for me. To interpret such feelings, we have to first be aware of them and be able to name them. The trouble is, many of us, especially us men, have a hard time identifying what we feel. When asked how we feel, we answer "good" or "bad" and the conversation ends there. The nuances and degrees of feeling are things we still need to learn. Intellectually we know of the difference in degree among frustration, anger, and rage, but can we say what each one feels like? For many of us, the world of our emotions is just opening up. Much learning is still required if we are to read the signs of God's guidance in our emotional lives.

As the mystery of our emotions suggests, much of what we communicate to ourselves and to each other is nonverbal. Some of that nonverbal information is processed consciously; however, most of it is taken in and deciphered in the half-conscious process of intuition. Though critical to our experience of the world, intuition is probably the most elusive of our inner functions. It takes subtle clues from the behavior of others and ourselves and makes split-second conclusions about the motives, causes, and perspectives involved. Intuition looks at a person of my acquaintance and says, "Trust him" or "Don't trust her." It helps us sort things out and protects us from deception and manipulation.

Though some people have a natural predisposition for making intuitive judgments, intuition is a skill and not a talent. It involves learning to discover the meaning below the surface, the messages behind the words, the motives behind the action. Most of us spend our lives learning how to use intuition without really knowing that we are doing it. Using it most effectively, however, requires paying attention to what is going on around us. It requires good interpersonal skills and experience in dealing with different kinds of people, so that I learn how to read the subtle nonverbal and tonal communication cues that send the silent messages that intuition receives.

As with the messages I receive from my emotions and from my head, intuition can be wrong. It is not infallible. Suppose I was taught to distrust people of a certain cultural or ethnic group. When a person from this group approaches me, I will go on the defensive. This is my intuition at work, but there is another name for it too: prejudice. As with our other internal cues, intuition is best trusted when the information it provides me is integrated with the rest of my inner functions. Prejudiced intuitions are more likely to be corrected when integrated with thoughtful reflection ("I don't really believe this") and reflection on our feelings ("Why do I feel so anxious all of a sudden?"). We make better decisions when we consider whether all our inner activities are pointing to the same conclusion. Beyond that, it is critically important to check our most important conclusions against other perspectives, especially those of people we respect and trust.

Checking the Wisdom Sources

When making big decisions, most of us bounce the options off a few friends first. With the biggest decisions, many people seek the counsel of the "wisdom figures" in their lives. It could be a teacher or business mentor. Maybe it's a parent or a priest or a friend whose experience of life is held in esteem. Whomever the wisdom sources are, it is itself a time-tested piece of spiritual wisdom to check with them. All of us need a reality check. Have I read all the signs well? Are there blind spots in my reasoning? Am I fooling myself? Have I really seen the "big picture" accurately? Asking questions such as these, we check our experience against that of wisdom figures present (a spiritual director or mentor) and those of the past (the wisdom of tradition). We check it against trusted fellow community members as well. Most of the dilemmas we face are not unique, and checking our conclusions against those of others can only help. Others' experience can give us both affirmation and critique to aid in our discernment. It is not that we should ask others to make our decisions *for* us. We take the advice of wisdom sources seriously, but in the end each of us must make the big decisions in life for himself or herself!

Discernment and Prayer

Discernment is really the art of discovering God's will for us. The process of discovery includes a great deal of self-discovery, of unveiling the person God has created me to be. Most of us think we know ourselves pretty well, and we do. Yet there is also much that is not clear. In this imperfect world, we cannot see anything, including ourselves, exactly as it is. Thus, just as we need to use a mirror to survey our physical selves, we need the instruments of self-study (intuition, reflection, and feeling) to see our interior selves. Naturally, these instruments will miss some things. Other people will see parts of us that we cannot, so we ask for their feedback. But only God, who sees and knows all, will see everything.

So it goes without saying that seeking help from God is a must for discernment. No big decision should be made without spending some time in prayer and reflection, placing our concerns before the Author of Life. Setting aside such moments in our lives prepares us to be open, to listen and watch, hoping to somehow hear God's voice in our lives. In prayer time, God may see fit to send us insights we have not realized thus far on our own—not in the sense of real material voices or of lightning messages from the blue, but in the way the Holy Spirit moves our minds and hearts and actions. God may give us a strong sense of either peace or upset. We may stumble upon an obvious insight that we have missed. Maybe we will be reminded of what is important. But even if God sends no earthshaking insight in prayer time, it is good to sit before the One who loves us and remember that we are not alone in the universe. While all things pass away, God remains. And God will never abandon us.

Being Human: Room to Maneuver, Hindsight, and the God of Second Chances

Hearing talk of God's will, some people begin to think of a monolithic entity, fixed from the beginning of time, indifferent to our needs and desires. Anyone who misreads it fails the test. How could there be second chances with the road of faith so clearly mapped and paved?

But when we think like this, we are really speaking of the will of the god of our fears, not the God of the scriptures. This is the will of the "anal-retentive god"—the remote, inflexible, rigid one, whose children are of little consequence. However we received this image of God, it is not accurate. The God who became human in Jesus of Nazareth is not so callous and remote. Our God is not amused by settling a heavy load on our backs. Jesus said, "Come to me, all you who labor and are burdened, and I will give you rest.... For my yoke is easy, and my burden light" (Mt 11:28). In fact, God wants what is best for us, for all people, and for all of creation. This God knows both the limits and the wonderful possibilities of our human situation and has chosen us as partners in redemption. This is the God who writes straight even with some of our most crooked human lines.

All of this should ease our minds a bit in considering the complex process of discernment. Given our human failings and limitations, it seems clear that not all our discernments will turn out for the best. Moreover, we will never know at the moment of choice whether or not our most well-discerned decisions are indeed God's will for us. We may be absolutely convinced that we have chosen God's will, yet end up choosing something that is bad for us and bad for others. As Thomas Merton writes in a well-known prayer, "The fact that I think I am doing your will does not mean that I am actually doing so." Hindsight, however, instructs us well if we are willing to risk looking back on what is done. Reflecting on our past discernments, we often have new eyes to see both our good decisions and our bad ones. Thus, hindsight has an important place in the process of discernment. Surveying the mistakes and successes of the past, we know better how to approach the future.

Still, even in hindsight, not all things can be seen clearly. Life inevitably involves interpretation, and interpretation can always be off. The good news is that the Holy Spirit dwells among us and guides us anyway. The point in human endeavors, as a friend of mine reminds me, is not to *succeed* but to *try* with all our hearts. God takes care of everything else. Thomas Merton finishes the above-mentioned prayer like this:

> But I believe that the desire to please you does in fact please you. And I hope I have that desire in all that I am doing.... And I know that if I do this you will lead me by the right road, though I may know nothing about it. Therefore I will trust you always...for you are ever with me, and you will never leave me to face my perils alone.[1]

Chapter Twelve: CONCLUSION—
EDITING GOD IN

Spirituality is our understanding of the relationship between God and human beings—us, that is. Throughout this book, we have explored that relationship, drawing on the experience of young adults (and some who have survived young adulthood and lived to tell about it) along the way. I hope these stories from the lives of people I have encountered have awakened the story of your spiritual life, of your relationship with God. I hope that the vignettes and ideas woven into the story of this book leave you feeling "Oh, yeah, I know what this guy's talking about," or at the very least, "Interesting idea, but he's way off base here. In my experience it's more like...."

Wherever each of us believes our road of faith banks and turns, we all pretty much agree that it's headed toward God. Everything, in the long run, has to relate back to the God of love—which is funny, in a way. In these pages, as in most of our lives, God often recedes into the background. We seldom speak of God when dealing with the concrete, everyday events of our lives, and these are the very events I have tried to focus on here. No one speaks of God and plumbing, of the divine plan in trigonometry, of discerning the Holy Spirit in your lovelife. Yet God is there, if slightly out of focus, an inch or two below the surface. Of course, we don't always have to say "God is present" to know that God is indeed present. But we still may want to be reminded of the many places God dwells in our lives. The following reminders are meant to help us put the God who is always present back into our perspective.

Editing God into Our Lives

There is no difference between our spiritual lives and the lives we live every day. This should be clear to us by now. God is the source and sustainer of all that is real; every thing and every moment exist as pure divine gift. This goes for Monday morning's breakfast, Renaissance art, and the life of every person that we love. If not for God, every part of our lives would vanish and ourselves as well. Thus, our spiritual lives (the phrase is a misnomer in one way) *are* our lives, our *real* lives.

The challenge, then, for people of faith is to "edit God into our lives," to remind ourselves of God's work in every part of our living. There is much compartmentalization in our lives. We sometimes act like God only steps in for an hour each Sunday or perhaps for the five minutes before bedtime. Yet deep inside us we know that God is present in every moment. The trick is to become more conscious of that fact and to welcome God into each moment of our day. The biggest way, of course, is to ensure that we set aside some prayer time every day, just as we set aside time for our families and friends.

But we can edit God into our work as well. We can admire the gifts that enable us to do the things we do. We can ascertain the reason for our work—training for the future, preparing to raise a family, paying the bills, serving other people, or just doing it for the sheer pleasure of doing what it is that we do—and fit that into our vision of where God is calling us. And why not offer our work itself to God—the products we make, the kindness and respect we offer to our co-workers, the moments of work themselves. This is a tough one for our culture, where we think of work as "that which I do that I don't like." But work has always been a part of the way people offered back to God the life that God has given them.

For those who are students, what about editing God into our study? In the Jewish tradition, *to study is to pray,* particularly when it comes to religious matters. But all matters are ultimately spiritual. Everything that is, points to God. In our tradition, we see no contradiction between science and faith, for science unravels the complexity of all things, inspiring awe in the person of faith. Nor do we find trouble in the arts, where the act of creation imitates that act of God. And the social sciences and humanities uncover the mysteries of being human, celebrating the image of God that we are. Not only is there no contradiction between so-called secular study and our faith, but they actually enhance one another. Faith gives to studies a sense of delight, awe, and gratitude. Secular study gives to faith new ideas and ways of thinking about reality. To expand to meet the demands of new frontiers of thought challenges our theology.

Finally, we can edit God into our worship. This sounds strange, but I have observed time and time again that it is necessary. I sometimes go through an entire liturgy without ever really thinking about the meaning of the ritual words. I do "mental laundry" and miss the scripture readings. I cannot remember the homily ten minutes afterward. I go through Sunday worship and forget to focus on the whole purpose of the event—God's relationship with the believing community. I suspect I am not the only one with this problem. True, some of it may be the quality of the worship service. But that is no excuse for our tuning out all the time. The same God that we have met in nature, in friendships, in all kinds of ways, is the God of our worship services as well.

Practicing Our Faith

We might also describe editing God into our lives as practicing our faith. Many of us have, often enough, heard terms like "practicing Catholic" or "practicing Lutheran" or perhaps just that "Oh, she practices her faith." But what do we mean by these phrases? Do we mean *practice* in the sense of "not a real game"? That is, "it's okay to *practice* at faith, but avoid involving it in real life." This kind of practice might mean attending worship services, not eating meat on Fridays in Lent, and jumping through all the prescribed religious hoops; but it would not mean getting involved in a faith community, going on retreat, letting the gospel challenge my sense of social responsibility for the poor. According to this sense of practice, we avoid entanglement in matters of spirituality. It's like relegating God to the sidelines!

Instead, God calls us to be "spiritual athletes." We are to practice our faith so that we might get good at it. First and foremost, this means taking the gospel to heart, allowing God's work in my life to move me, to change me. It means continual conversion. It probably also means involvement in a faith community, seeking direction in our lives, committing ourselves to treating all human beings with respect. With this practice, I am in the game for real. I have to act on my faith, to work for social justice. It's also a kind of spiritual calisthenics—I really have to keep at it to keep growing.

What Is God Doing Here?

We are all quite comfortable with the presence of God at worship, in the beauty of a sunset, in the warmth of a friend or loved one's hug. Harder to deal with are the unexpected and ironic ways that God breaks into our lives. Yet that seems God's favorite way of showing us divine love and power. Scripture holds countless examples—the elderly and childless Abraham and Sarah become parents to "descendants as countless as the stars of the sky," (Gn 22:17); the youngest and most inconsequential of the sons of Jesse is chosen to be King of Israel (1 Sm 16:1–13); the brutal enemies of Israel, the Ninevites, repent of their sin and receive God's forgiveness (the book of Jonah); Jesus declares that the poor and the hungry, the dregs of society, are actually the most blessed in the eyes of God (Lk 6:20–21); the murderous and persecuting Saul becomes the great Paul, apostle to the Gentiles (Galatians, Acts). Taken as a whole, these stories suggest to us that God prefers the unpopular and unexpected route, the way that shatters our false images of how things ought to be.

And so we watch for God's ironic breaking into our world We toss out expectations and prepare ourselves for some discomfort and confusion. The God of love comes to us as comforter and maternal caregiver (Is 46:3–4) but also comes as the One who kicks us in the behind. When my "party summer" after college graduation was interrupted by eviction from the apartment I was subletting, I took it as a sign that I had better start seriously looking for a job. A friend of mine got an uncomfortable wake-up call from God when the husband she had been very dependent upon was suddenly incapacitated by a serious illness. She found herself called to be more independent and to allow someone else to depend on her.

God's ironic ways of speaking to us are legion. We may find divine reminders coming to us from people we do not like, from atheists and agnostics, from family members we resent, from people whose lives are more messed up than ours. And then there are the messages themselves. God dreams dreams for us that we would not choose, presents futures more wonderful and more difficult than we would have imagined. I know a woman who left her lucrative law practice to become a high school teacher. Several parents and not a few members of Catholic religious orders have admitted to me that if they had known what their choice of lifestyle would entail, they would have run away! But this is our God of surprises, the God who finds a way to us even in the most menial activities of life. (I have a friend who insists that God gets him parking places!) The God of irony is always working in mysterious ways, accomplishing things with a rhythm and sense of time none of us understands. We can only pray for patience and a broad enough sense of humor to appreciate and deal with it.

God Is Our Friend

A woman once put the question to God, "When you look at me, what do you see?" God's response came back without hesitation: "More than anything else, I see one that I love."

The final and ultimate goal of life is intimacy with God. God loves us "beyond all telling" and wants to befriend us. It was for this purpose that God created us, and there is no greater joy or happiness. Thus, as we have intimated in chapters past, the road of faith becomes a lifelong lesson in friendship. We spend our whole lives learning to love people in order that we might truly love God with all our heart, all our mind, and all our strength. When we have learned to do that, then we will be complete and full people.

Our awareness that intimate friendship with the triune God is the long-range plan of all existence can put certain things into perspective. If we are going to spend eternity in relationship with God, literally living with God, then integrating God into the fullness of our lives *now* is a number one priority. Eternity begins now. Salvation begins now, not after we die.

In addition, if we truly trust this God that wishes to be friends with us, our best course of action is to allow God to take the lead in our lives. We are still each of us responsible for our lives, to be sure, but we are not responsible for our ultimate salvation. We can "let go" of our need to control everything in our lives and "let God" take over. In effect, we seek to become partners with God, to become a part of God's plan of salvation for the whole world. This is easier said than done, of course. But we can begin to do this, and over time it will get easier. It will begin to seem natural to "strive first for the kingdom of God and God's righteousness" (Mt 6:33), for our trust in God will grow as we agree to surrender our lives.

As we grow in our awareness of God our Friend's immense love for us, we will also stop clobbering ourselves for not being perfect. We are *not* perfect, and we never will be. When we make mistakes, when we sin, when we hurt God and other people, God's love for us is no less. Our Loving God forgives us and calls us to try again, to avoid making the same mistakes, but not to feel ten inches tall. We are of infinite worth in the eyes of the Lord. Our basic worth is based on the life that God gave us, not on what we do. God invites us to take half of the time that we normally use for fault-finding self-analysis and instead use it to remind ourselves of God's great kindness and mercy.

God Is Our Navigator

Our lives are journeys, road trips. That much is clear by now. These journeys move us ever closer to a more mature faith. We travel down a route familiar to us in some parts, unfamiliar in others. We choose some of our companions;

others come to us without our consent. We are charged with keeping our vehicles in shape, with collecting the right supplies, with trying to avoid some of the meaner obstacles. We learn along the way, growing in our understanding of the route and sharing our education with our companions. Sometimes the car stalls, and we are stuck for a while. Other times, we even crash and suffer the consequences. Whatever happens along the road of faith, we can be certain of one thing. There are good things on the road ahead; there is hope. We can be sure because of the trust we have in God. God, the transcendent navigator, loved us into being and is arranging each mile of our trip in partnership with us. This God will never let us down.

Notes

CHAPTER THREE

1. Amateur theologian's note: Of course, the courage that we need to respond to God's grace is itself a gift from God. It's important to note because the Reformation started over things like this.

CHAPTER FOUR

1. Father Edward Malloy, C.S.C., "Study of Alcohol Abuse on Campus," *Origins,* 24, no. 6 (1994): 84–85.
2. If a person is truly addicted to love or to sex, that person needs to seek the help of a professional counselor or to attend twelve-step meetings, such as Sex and Love Addicts Anonymous (SLAA).

CHAPTER SIX

1. Mihaly Csikszentmihalyi, *Flow: The Psychology of Optimal Experience* (New York: HarperPerennial, 1991), 37.

CHAPTER EIGHT

1. Rainer Maria Rilke, *Letters to a Young Poet,* rev. ed., trans. M. D. Herter (New York: W.W. Norton, 1954), 18–19.

CHAPTER NINE

1. Two such books are recommended in the appendix of spiritual readings. Other recommended authors include Joseph Fitzmyer, Raymond Brown, Stanley Morrow, John Meier, and Elizabeth Schüssler Fiorenza. Lawrence Boadt's *Reading the Old Testament* (New York: Paulist, 1984) and Pheme Perkins' *Reading the New Testament* (New York: Paulist, 1988) both make fine introductory readings for those serious about Bible study.

CHAPTER ELEVEN

1. Thomas Merton, "The Road Ahead," from *Thoughts in Solitude* (New York: Farrar, Straus, 1958), quoted in *Thomas Merton: Spiritual Master,* ed. Lawrence S. Cunningham (New York: Paulist, 1992), 243.

Appendix: Recommended Spiritual Reading

Au, S.J., Wilkie. *By Way of the Heart: Toward a Holistic Christian Spirituality.* New York: Paulist, 1989.

Barry, S.J., William A. *God and You: Prayer as a Personal Relationship.* New York: Paulist, 1987.

Bellah, Robert, and others. *Habits of the Heart: Individualism and Commitment in American Life.* Berkeley: University of California Press, 1985. Also, *The Good Society.* New York: Alfred A. Knopf, 1991.

Buechner, Frederick. *Telling the Truth: The Gospel as Tragedy, Comedy, and Fairy Tale.* San Francisco: Harper & Row, 1977.

Coffin, William Sloan. *The Courage to Love.* San Francisco: Harper & Row, 1984.

* Csikszentmihalyi, Mihaly. *Flow: The Psychology of Optimal Experience.* New York: Harper Perennial, 1991.

de Mello, Anthony. *Sadhana: A Way to God—Christian Exercises in Eastern Form.* Garden City, N.Y.: Image Books, 1984. Also *The Song of the Bird.* Garden City, N.Y.: Image Books, 1984. Nearly anything by de Mello is valuable.

* Dreyer, Elizabeth. *Earth Crammed with Heaven: A Spirituality of Everyday Life.* New York: Paulist, 1994.

Edwards, Tilden. *Spiritual Friend: Reclaiming the Gift of Spiritual Direction.* New York: Paulist, 1980.

* Endo, Shusaku. *A Life of Jesus.* New York: Paulist, 1977.

Fox, Matthew. *Creation Spirituality: Liberating Gifts for the Peoples of the Earth.* San Francisco: HarperSanFrancisco, 1991.

Fujita, Neil S. *Introducing the Bible.* New York: Paulist, 1981.

Hays, Edward. *Pray All Ways.* Easton, Kans.: Forest of Peace Books, Inc., 1981. Also *St. George and the Dragon and the Search for the Holy Grail.* Easton, Kans.: Forest of Peace Books, Inc., 1986.

Heschel, Abraham. *God in Search of Man: A Philosophy of Judaism.* New York: Harper & Row, 1955.

*Merton, Thomas. *Spiritual Direction and Meditation.* Collegeville, Minn.: Liturgical Press, 1960. Also *New Seeds of Contemplation.* New York:

New Directions, 1962. *Thoughts in Solitude.* New York: Farrar & Straus, 1958. *Thomas Merton, Spiritual Master,* ed. Lawrence S. Cunningham. New York: Paulist, 1992. *Praying the Psalms.* Collegeville, Minn.: Liturgical Press, 1956. *Raids on the Unspeakable.* New York: New Directions, 1966. Anything by Thomas Merton is good spiritual reading.

Morrow, Stanley. *The Words of Jesus in Our Gospels.* New York: Paulist, 1979.

Nouwen, Henri J. M. *Intimacy: Essays in Pastoral Psychology.* San Francisco: HarperSanFrancisco, 1969. Also *The Wounded Healer: Ministry in Contemporary Society.* New York: Doubleday, 1972.

Peck, F. Scott. *The Road Less Travelled.* New York: Touchstone, 1978. Popular as they are, I'm not a fan of Peck's other books.

Richo, David. *How To Be An Adult: A Handbook on Psychological and Spiritual Integration.* New York: Paulist, 1991.

Rock, S.J., Leo. *Making Friends with Yourself: Christian Growth and Self-Acceptance.* New York: Paulist, 1990.

* Stindl-Rast, Brother David. *Gratefulness, the Heart of Prayer: An Approach to Life in Fullness.* New York: Paulist, 1984.

Ulanov, Ann and Barry. *Primary Speech: A Psychology of Prayer.* Atlanta: John Knox Press, 1982.

* Vanier, Jean. *Community and Growth,* rev. ed. New York: Paulist, 1989.

* Walker, Alice. *The Color Purple.* New York: Washington Square Press, 1982.

Westley, Richard. *Redemptive Intimacy.* Mystic, Conn.: Twenty-third Publications, 1980.

Whitehead, Evelyn and James. *Christian Life Patterns.* New York: Doubleday, 1979.

* Specially Recommended

Readings on Codependence and Addiction

Alcoholics Anonymous: The Story of How Many Thousands of Men and Women Have Recovered from Alcoholism, 3rd ed. New York: AA World Services, 1976. This is the famous "big book" of Alcoholics Anonymous.

Beattie, Melody. *Codependent No More.* San Francisco: HarperCollins, 1987.

Crosby, Michael. *The Dysfunctional Church: Addiction and Codependency in the Family of Catholicism.* Notre Dame, In.: Ave Maria, 1991.

Schaef, Anne Wilson. *Co-dependence: Misunderstood—Misdiagnosed.* San Francisco: Harper & Row, 1985. Also *Escape from Intimacy: The Pseudo-Relationship Addictions.* San Francisco: Harper & Row, 1989.